do it

Planning and Fitting
Kitchens

GUILD OF
MASTER CRAFTSMAN
PUBLICATIONS

Dennis Dixon

First published 2007 by

Guild of Master Craftsman Publications Ltd.
Castle Place, 166 High Street, Lewes, East Sussex BN7 1XU

Copyright in the Work © GMC Publications 2007

ISBN 978-1-86108-498-9

A catalogue record for this book is available from the British Library.

Photographic acknowledgements on page 171.

Production Manager Jim Bulley
Managing Editor Gerrie Purcell
Editor Rachel Netherwood
Managing Art Editor Gilda Pacitti

Set in Clarendon and Meta Plus
Colour origination by Altaimage
Printed and bound by Sino Publishing

Planning and Fitting
Kitchens

Contents

Introduction

The chance to plan and fit a new kitchen will probably be a rare experience for most people. When the opportunity arises, avoid being seduced by the latest gadgets and hi-tech appliances, look beyond the showroom appeal of the cabinets, and instead give the planning stages the importance your kitchen deserves.

A new kitchen is, after all, a long-term investment, often not replaced for twenty years. Increasingly, it is the natural place for family and friends to congregate – the heart of the home. Studies have shown that many families spend as much as 40% of their time in the kitchen. For these two reasons alone, when contemplating a new kitchen, it is has to be worthwhile starting out on the fundamentals of the design. The investment in time spent at the planning stage will be repaid many times over.

Planning and Fitting Kitchens is an up to date and comprehensive guide to lead you from the first planning decisions through to completion.

You will benefit from my years of hands-on experience in the planning as well as the practical side of kitchen fitting. The book will explain what to do and when, how to use special tools, the materials required and how to avoid the pitfalls of a particular course of action. It is set out in a logical progression and, to make it easy to use, each stage is supported by step-by-step pictures and clear diagrams. There are numerous tricks of the trade to help you achieve a truly professional finish.

But the book will undoubtedly have wider appeal. By understanding 'what, where, when and how', anyone contemplating changing their kitchen will be able to make informed decisions in order to save time and money. Even if you only want to install a washing machine, the book will pay for itself.

Furthermore, the book will be of great benefit to budding kitchen fitters. Existing tradesmen wishing to diversify as well as young people entering the trade should find the book an extremely useful guide. The sections dealing with specialist tools will enable you to develop your skills and the guidelines will provide an invaluable source of reference.

Only you can know what kind of kitchen you need, and that is why this book puts you in the driving seat: it will show you how to bring your own ideas to life, not just copy someone else's.

CAUTION POWER TOOL SAFETY

If an accident is going to happen, with power tools it will happen fast. It is obviously important to take precautions – not only to avoid injury to oneself and others but also to avoid damage to tools and materials. Whilst each machine or tool has its own idiosyncrasies there are, nevertheless, general safety procedures that are common to all, and any person who engages in DIY would be wise to become familiar with these to the point where they are second nature.

■ Do not wear loose clothing or jewellery and if necessary tie back long hair (below). Anything that could get caught up in moving parts is an accident waiting to happen.

■ Do not operate machinery when tired, drunk or taking medication.

■ Use appropriate protective wear. In most operations involving power tools there is likely to be debris thrown off so wear some form of eye shield (below right). If the job involves dust, wear a dust mask. Working with machines can be noisy

so wear some form of ear protection: ear defenders or simple earplugs. 'Use it or lose it!' is a simple safety slogan that should not be ignored.

■ The work area should be dry, clean, well lit and tidy. There should not be anything to cause a trip or a slip. Children and pets must be kept out of the way.

■ Inspect tools regularly for signs of wear and damage. Look for scorch marks, loose screws, nicks in the cable, exposed wires and so on. Check that motor air slots are clean and free of debris (above). Cutting edges must be sharp. Blade guards must operate properly.

■ Avoid unintentional starting. Power tools should be unplugged when not in use, particularly when making adjustments and changing accessories or attachments. Do not carry them with a finger on the trigger (or by holding the cable).

■ Use sensible techniques. Either the tool or the work must be secure. When force is applied through a hand-held tool to an unsteady work piece there is a good chance that something will slip, causing injury or damage.

■ Check that the path of the cut is clear of obstruction, including the hidden side. Make sure the cable is out of harm's way. For hand-held power tools drape it over the shoulder (below).

■ Take a firm stance, cut away from the body and do not overreach.

■ Wait until the motor of a power tool reaches full speed before applying it to the work piece.

■ Always adhere to manufacturers' instructions.

■ Stay alert, use common sense and do not take risks.

1

Kitchen Planning

It is important to consider how your new kitchen will be used. Following a few simple guidelines will enable you to make the most of the space available and produce a kitchen that not only looks good but also serves your needs – a kitchen that will be a pleasure to work in.

Lifestyle Considerations

Every household is somewhat unique. The size, make-up, ages, culture and habits will have implications on your kitchen plan. Your lifestyle may require the kitchen to double up as, for example, a dining area, crèche, office, greenhouse, TV room, hobby area or pet's dormitory. Dining could range from simple children's meals through to formal dinner parties. These considerations will not only affect the allocation of space but will also have an impact on the choice of equipment.

Making a 'lifestyle audit' (see box opposite) is a good starting point for planning your ideal kitchen.

FIND A SPACE
A kitchen can be planned to fit neatly into a compact space *(left)* freeing up room for an alternative use. This would be quite adequate for those who don't spend much time in it but if you have a growing family and like to spend time cooking together then a larger area would be more appropriate *(above)*. Knocking two rooms into one to create an open-plan living space may be the answer.

✳ A Lifestyle Audit

✔ **SIZE OF FAMILY (current and future)**
Extra or less space may need to be allocated

✔ **SPECIAL REQUIREMENTS FOR DISABILITIES**
Consider non-standard dimensions for units and floor space

✔ **CULTURAL/RELIGIOUS REQUIREMENTS**
Special cooking and food preparation features

✔ **FREQUENCY/STYLE OF ENTERTAINING**
Size of preparation area/cooking facilities

✔ **MEALS IN KITCHEN**
Snacks at a breakfast bar or full meals at the table?

✔ **DOES COOKING INVOLVE ONE OR MORE PEOPLE?**
Spacial relationships (see page 13)

✔ **MEAL PREPARATION AND SHOPPING FREQUENCY**
Type of storage (see page 25)

✔ **IS THE PRIMARY USER RIGHT- OR LEFT-HANDED?**
Flow direction (see page 20)

✔ **ALTERNATIVE USE OF THE ROOM**
Electrical, TV, telephone facilities

FLEXI-WORKING
Consider how you might want to use the kitchen at different times. A spacious island unit *(below)* can be a breakfast bar for occasional meals as well as a food preparation area, while a dining table *(bottom)* provides extra desk space for home study or a formal entertaining area.

The Existing Kitchen

Replacing a kitchen provides an opportunity to rectify fundamental problems. If the kitchen area has an awkward shape, such as doors in inconvenient places, or is simply too small, logically this would be the sensible time to sort out any physical limitations. In any case, it is a good idea to take a moment to 'think outside the box' before becoming embroiled in the details.

A Suitable Space

The starting point should always be the existing kitchen: how far does it meet your current and future requirements? Question whether it is too small/too big, too long/too short, too narrow/too wide. Perhaps the existing layout could be changed to make more of a garden view?

Think about the elements that work and those that cause frustration. Sometimes it helps to visualize the tasks that are done and follow them through in sequences. For example, meal preparation will involve taking food from the fridge, freezer or a cupboard to a preparation area. This may be followed by the use of a chopping board, utensils, a pan, water and then the hob. It can be irritating if things are not to hand when needed. A simple reorganization could make the kitchen a much more pleasant place in which to work.

KNOCKED THROUGH
In this house *(below)* additional space has been found by removing the wall between the hallway and kitchen. Even the space under the stairs has been opened up and now houses kitchen units.

5 Ideas for Alternative Spaces

TAKE OVER Check out the adjoining areas to see if any space could be more usefully employed in the kitchen. Older houses in particular can have small rooms that have long since become redundant. For example, there may be an old outside WC or a scullery that could be incorporated (also providing an alternative drain).

UTILITIZE Perhaps there is a small room that could be comandeered as a utility room for the laundry appliances, thereby freeing up valuable space in the kitchen.

CHANGE PLACES A radical option may be to consider a room swap. Could, for example, the dining room become the kitchen and the kitchen be converted into a new dining room? What about the garage? The chances are that it could become a habitable room without too much upheaval.

OPEN UP A contemporary solution is to knock through between the kitchen and the dining room to create an open-plan living concept. This could be a practical solution for growing families.

VENTURE OUTDOORS Finally, having explored all the internal possibilities look outside. There may be room to extend the kitchen. Even a simple conservatory could provide sufficient space for a stylish play/dining area.

A well-planned kitchen is a pleasure to work in. Here, an island unit is the ideal solution for a busy family: they can access the surface from all sides without getting in each other's way and talk to each other while they are working. The sink and hob unit are both nearby, while a large trolley moves plates and cutlery easily between the washing-up area and the dining room.

Work Relations

This process will help assess whether the relationships between working areas are correct. For example, perhaps the cutlery drawer is too far from the drainer. Perhaps a right-handed person may find it more comfortable to wash up from left to right. What relationship should the dishwasher have to the sink? Are the wall cupboards too high or too low? When someone else is in the kitchen are there points of congestion? If it is tiring to work in the old kitchen, is this because it is too big or is there something wrong with the layout? Check out *Positioning Hobs and Cookers* on page 24.

Finally, do not forget that other members of the household may have useful suggestions. Involvement at this stage will help bring them 'on-side' when they have to put up with the disruption that the change-over will inevitably cause.

Case Study 1: The First-time Buyers' Kitchen

This kitchen forms part of a late Victorian property that was converted into flats in the 1960s. The existing layout poses lots of problems. There is insufficient storage and a lack of work surfaces and the location of the washing machine by the sink means that the kitchen door cannot be closed. Not only that, but the units are old and and dated and the wiring and cooker are unsafe. But the room is light and bright, with plenty of potential. With some careful planning even a small kitchen, such as this one, can be beautiful.

The owners want to make better use of space in order to incorporate a dining area. They also want plenty of storage, which will mean adding more wall units. The best way to incorporate these into the kitchen is to include the units, sink and cooker on a single wall (see page 21). A table can then be fitted under the window, increasing the use of natural light (see right).

As first-time buyers, the owners can't afford an expensive refurbishment. One way of saving money is to do as much of the work as possible themselves. Another way to cut costs is use recycled materials – such as a reclaimed worktop or second-hand units – and to buy nearly new appliances. There are lots of ways to get the kitchen you want without spending a lot of money (see page 16). The finished kitchen is on page 166.

(Above) The existing kitchen has been cobbled together, which is a common feature of badly converted properties. These old, mismatched units will be removed to make way for the appliances and new cabinets.

(Below) This extension socket has no on/off switch, which is unsafe as well as impractical. It is also the only electric point in the kitchen.

(Above) Half the window frame has been removed to make way for a tiled splashback. This looks unattractive and also blocks out a lot of natural light – 45cm of the window is covered up. The owners will remove the splashback to make the most of the natural light and then restore the original Victorian frame.

(Above) Fitting a new kitchen provides the perfect opportunity to upgrade appliances. This old cooker is faulty and unsafe and will be replaced with an integrated, stainless steel oven and hob.

(Below) The sink is perched upon a central unit and an unstable end panel. The location of the washing machine means that the door cannot be closed.

How Much will it Cost?

Most of us are forced to juggle our various needs with limited resources. A new kitchen is a serious expense and, before going too far, compare what you would like to do with how much you can comfortably afford, now and over time.

Whilst you ponder over financial constraints consider the question of prudence. If you intend to stay in the same house for the foreseeable future then £12,000 may be a reasonable investment. However, for someone looking to move in a few months' time this level of expense may not be fully recoverable. In this situation a quick face-lift may be more appropriate.

top tip*

A functional kitchen is a necessity but they are marketed as luxuries and it is easy to get carried away. Try to be realistic. Allocate your budget between the three main cost areas: cabinets, appliances and building work.

Calling in the Professionals

Using some tradesmen can be expensive. If the plan requires appliances to be relocated do not underestimate the cost of moving services such as gas, water and electrics. Likewise, the cost of a simple alteration need not be daunting but as soon as the work involves structural changes, be prepared for the additional expense of professional services.

Expensive Tastes

Bespoke, one-off pieces will cost a lot more than mass produced items. Granite and Corian, which are tailor-made to fit, will set you back a lot more than an off-the-shelf laminate worktop. Similarly, the very latest in all-singing all-dancing appliances will eat into the budget at an alarming rate so do not be tempted by technology.

✳ Make your Money Go Further

✔ Check out local joinery works before going to an expensive showroom. You may find one that will copy a top-of-the-range design for a fraction of the price.

✔ A simple face-lift may be all that is required. If the basic carcasses are in good condition consider refreshing the doors and drawer fronts with a couple of coats of paint.

✔ The doors and drawer fronts could be replaced with modern equivalents, saving a considerable amount of time and money compared with renewing the whole units. Finish these off with new handles to create a contemporary look.

✔ In many instances the old laminate worktops could be replaced with new ones. A little more effort is required but the result would be a brand new look and the chance to transform the colour scheme.

✔ Use open shelves instead of wall units. DIY superstores offer wide ranges at affordable prices. Clever arrangements can be made to look stylish.

✔ If your existing appliances are still in good shape but your budget is not, reinstall them for now with the intention of replacing them later when finances allow.

✔ Check out auctions, fairs, local papers and car boot sales for items suitable for stripping and recycling. Pick up inexpensive kitchenware at the same time.

✔ Use freestanding units and appliances and take them with you when you move home.

✔ Look on the internet for appliances at discount prices (see page 170 for some suppliers).

MAKE AN INITIAL BUDGET LIST

With a rough idea of your perfect kitchen in mind you can start to make a full list of your requirements and calculate how much it could all cost. Remember to list everything – not only the kitchen units, worktops and appliances but also the surface treatments such as tiles and paint. You can then go on to identify the style of kitchen you want (see pages 34–39) and find a kitchen that will match your style and budget. When everything has been listed and costed you will have a yardstick for comparison as you shop around. The following budget checklist may be useful.

Kitchen units

Carcasses, doors and drawers ....£_____
Trim (plinth, cornice, pelmet)........................£_____
End panels ....£_____
Handles ....£_____
Accessories (baskets, pull-outs, shelves) ......£_____
Worktops, bolts and end-laminate................£_____

Appliances

Oven...£_____
Hob ....£_____
Extractor/re-circulator.................................£_____
Sink and waste...£_____
Tap ....£_____
Dishwasher ....£_____
Washing machine ....£_____
Tumble dryer ....£_____
Fridge ....£_____
Freezer ....£_____
Microwave ....£_____
Water softener ....£_____
Waste disposer ....£_____

Lighting

Ceiling..£_____
Cabinet...£_____
Transformers ....£_____

Sundries

Plumbing:
  waste pipe, traps, fittings ....£_____
  water pipe and fittings ....£_____
Electrical:
  cables...£_____
  accessories...£_____
Miscellaneous:
  screws, adhesives, plaster, wall plugs ....£_____
  fillers, tape, brackets, battening, etc. ....£_____
Ventilation:
  trunking or duct, grills.................................£_____

Tools

Purchase ....£_____
Hire ....£_____
Safety wear ....£_____

Surface treatments

Plaster..£_____
Wall tiles, adhesive and grout......................£_____
Floor tiles, adhesive and grout.....................£_____
Paint ....£_____

Building works

Materials ....£_____
Labour ....£_____

Fees

L A Planning Permission................................£_____
L A Building Control ....£_____

Professional help

Builder ....£_____
Electrician (Part P registered) ....£_____
Plumber (Corgi registered)...........................£_____
Kitchen fitter ....£_____
Decorator ....£_____
Architect ....£_____
Surveyor ....£_____

Subtotal ....£_____

Contingency allowance

add 10% ....£_____

Total ....£_____

MAKE A ROOM PLAN

Before the kitchen can be designed it is necessary, of course, to make a plan of the room. The following stages could equally be applied to planning any room in the house. Whether it is a bathroom, kitchen or garden shed the process is the same.

1 Take a sheet of squared paper and sketch in the shape of the room filling the page. The drawing should be roughly in proportion but not to scale. Mark any permanent features such as windows and doors, radiators, boxed-in pipes and boiler **A**.

2 Measure accurately the length of each wall as well as the diagonal measurements of the room. Measure the widths of each window, door and other features and the distances to the corners **B**. Carefully mark these measurements on the rough sketch; preferably in millimetres. Finally, record any significant heights such as the ceiling, the height to the underside of a windowsill, the height of the boiler and, if it is wall-hanging, the free space below.

3 Now it is possible to make an accurate plan. If the diagonal lengths are equal then you will know that the walls are square. Lightly draw in the walls on a fresh piece of squared paper using a pencil and ruler **C**. Use the lines printed on the paper to get the correct alignment: walls parallel and corners at right angles. It is best to use a scale of 1 : 20 (1mm = 20mm). If you do not have a scale ruler then divide each of your measurements by 20 for the right distance to draw.

4 In the same way draw in the permanent features. If any doors open into the room, the swing of the door should be marked using a compass and the door shown in the open position **D**.

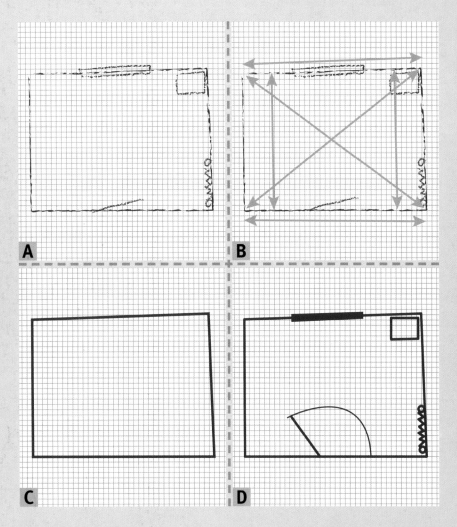

A

B

C

D

DRAW IRREGULAR WALLS ON YOUR PLAN

do it

1 Assuming the room forms a rectangle, take the longest wall – wall **1** – and draw this to length at the bottom of your plan.

2 Using a compass, set off the length of the adjacent wall (wall **2**: 2700mm) **A**.

3 From the other end of wall **1** set off the diagonal measurement – 4480mm – with the compass **B**. The point where compass arcs **A** and **B** cross is the other end of wall **2**.

4 Similarly, construct wall **3**. Draw an arc to the length of wall **3**: 2870mm **C**. Draw an arc to the length of the diagonal measurement: 4570mm **D**.

5 Join up the distance between the two sets of crossed arcs to complete wall **4**.

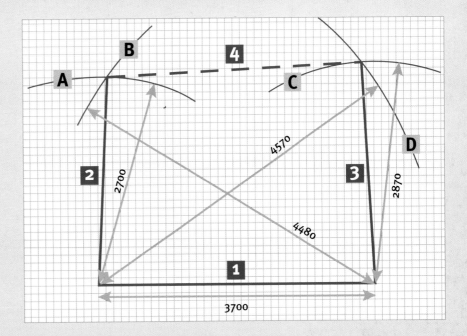

If the room is a more complicated shape, such as L-shaped, then this use of trigonometry is very useful. All you need to do is measure the distance to each corner from at least two fixed points. This will entail two or more extra diagonal measurements. The room is then constructed using the compass in the same way as a series of triangles.

Add the Plan Symbols

Once the room plan has been accurately drawn then add the services. It is worth recording the position of the gas pipe, waste outlet, stopcock, hot and cold vertical pipework, electric sockets, switches and so on. The following are standard plan symbols used by kitchen planners:

△	single socket (existing)	OWWWWO	radiator
▲	single socket (new)	WDU	waste disposal unit
△△	double socket (existing)	D/W	dishwasher
◼	30A cooker box	W/M	washing machine
CB	30A cooker box	ESP	end support panel
●	one-way light switch	BDE	base decor end panel
✗	two-way light switch	WDE	wall decor end panel
O	ceiling light outlet	TWDE	tall wall decor end panel
⊢—⊣	wall unit strip light	CBU	corner base unit
✳	12v halogen light	TLU	tall larder unit
Ⓢ	SSP (soil stack pipe)	BDPK	base drawer pack
●	waste pipe	T/S	tray slide
○ ●	hot/cold water pipes	T/R	towel rail
X	stopcock (elevation view)	int.	integrated
O	stopcock (plan view)	FZR	freezer
◑g	gas pipe	FR	refrigerator

Layout Concepts

BIN THERE, DONE THAT
A well-planned kitchen means an efficient production line. Here, the compost bin is conveniently placed in a cupboard beneath the sink. This makes it quicker and easier to dispose of kitchen waste during food preparation.

Activities carried out in a kitchen involve bending, lifting, reaching, walking and carrying: not too dissimilar to a light workout in a gym. By shortening the distances travelled and movements involved the amount of exertion will be reduced and kitchen work will be more enjoyable.

As far back as the mid-ninteenthth century the ergonomics of domestic kitchens were beginning to be considered. However, it was not until 1922 that a string study carried out by Christine Fredericks proved that the layout of kitchen furniture made a huge difference to the distances travelled and time spent carrying out routine kitchen chores. From these and later studies three concepts emerged.

The Production Line

Preparing a meal involves a sequence of events that starts with unpacking the shopping and ends with the washing up. In between there is storage, preparation, cooking, dishing up and serving. If the kitchen can be arranged to accommodate these tasks in the order that they occur this will enable a smooth flow of events which will ultimately save time and energy. When your initial plan is complete check its efficiency against your particular 'production line'. A study by Blum shows that by reorganizing the layout in a sample L-shaped kitchen, the distance travelled could be reduced by 20%.

Work Centres

To really improve the kitchen's efficiency consider each activity in its own right. Each stage of the meal will have its own requirements as to equipment, storage, work surface and so on. Visualize carrying out one of these stages standing still. For example, the preparation of a particular dish may require scales, a chopping board, utensils, bowls, condiments and lots of other ingredients. Imagine that you are not allowed to move your feet: everything you need would have to be within arm's reach. A 'work centre' of this nature would save a lot of walking and bending. Tasks could be done more quickly and with less effort. The work would be more enjoyable.

toptip*

Right-handed people generally feel more comfortable working clockwise and left-handed people prefer anti-clockwise. Relate the flow diagram to your new kitchen plan with this in mind.

To accommodate our production line we would need a series of 'work centres'. In a domestic kitchen this would not be practical. Work centres have to share work surfaces but by fitting them together in the correct sequence we can retain the basic production-line principle.

The Work Triangle

The concept of the work triangle was devised in the USA in the 1950s as a way of testing the practicality of kitchens in government-financed housing. The concept was so successful that it became regarded as fundamental to kitchen design and is still quoted in nearly every article written on this subject.

The triangle is formed by a line drawn from the refrigerator to the hob, then to the sink and back again to the refrigerator. When measured this line should not be more than 7m and not less than 3.6m. The lines of the triangle represent the walking routes backwards and forwards and cover the area where most of the work will take place. Obviously, the larger the triangle the more steps are needed to get things done. It makes sense to keep the triangle within the 7m limit in order to save time and promote safe working practice. Often, the larger the kitchen the more problematic this becomes.

top tip*

In practice, most journeys are between the cooker and the main work centre and from the main work centre to the sink and back again. There are significantly fewer trips to the food storage area. It is good practice to allow for a clear length of worktop within a step or two of the cooker and the sink and this will become the natural place to work.

Standard Layouts

There are five basic arrangements used to describe kitchen layouts but in practice the choice will be governed by the size and shape of your room and the position of doors and windows.

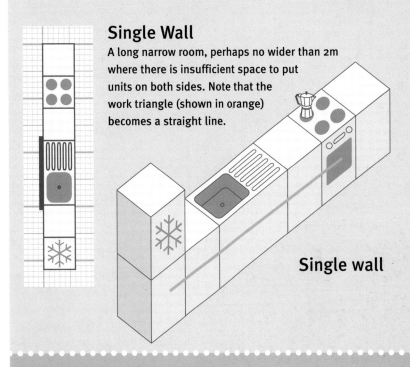

Single Wall
A long narrow room, perhaps no wider than 2m where there is insufficient space to put units on both sides. Note that the work triangle (shown in orange) becomes a straight line.

Single wall

Galley
Another long narrow room, probably with a door at each end, but wide enough to put units down parallel sides. This will create an excellent work triangle but there is a potential safety hazard from people crossing the work area to move between the two doors.

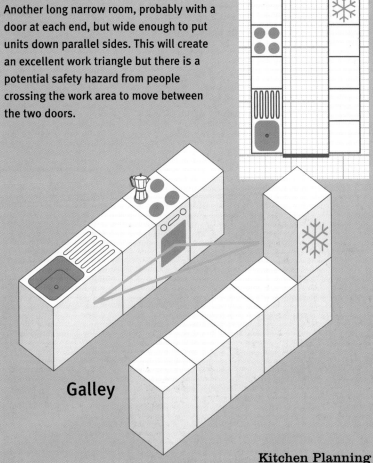

Galley

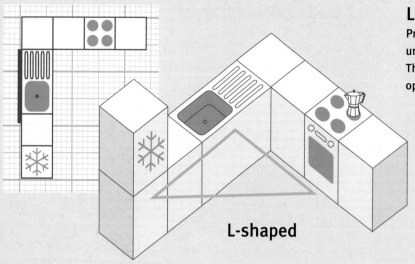

L-shaped
Probably a room with adjacent doors allowing units to be placed along two adjoining sides. There may be room for a dining area in the opposite corner.

L-shaped

U-shaped
This can produce a very efficient work triangle if the space is not obstructed. A small U-shaped area will only enable one person to work.

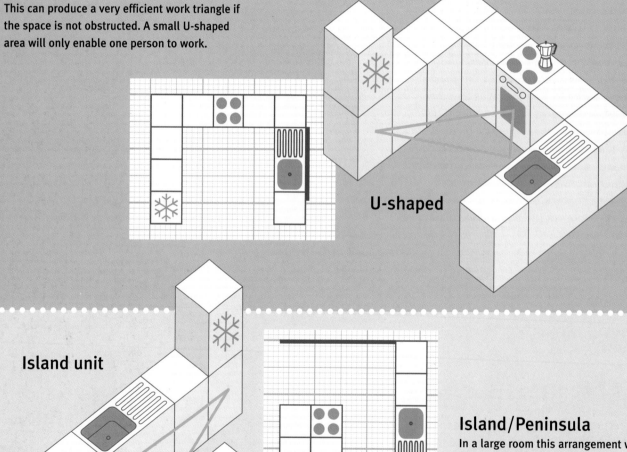

U-shaped

Island unit

Island/Peninsula
In a large room this arrangement will help compact the work triangle. An island can act as a central work station, linking the sides of the triangle. A peninsula can double up as a breakfast bar or a barrier to direct through-traffic away from the work area.

Developing the Kitchen Plan

You can now start to add more specific details to your plan. Start a new version of the plan by drawing a faint line 600mm out from all the walls with gaps left for the doors. This represents the edge of an imaginary standard worktop and will indicate the maximum layout that can be achieved. The line should then be adjusted to take account of space restrictions and incursions. This exercise will provide the basic framework in which to arrange the appliances and kitchen units.

Appliances

The task of arranging the appliances can be simplified by representing each one with a cardboard cutout. This will enable different arrangements to be tried out quickly, without spoiling the plan. Do this to the same scale as the drawing: 1:20.

Fortunately, most modern appliances are designed to fit into spaces 600mm wide. Fridges, freezers, single and double ovens, standard hobs, dishwashers, washing machines and dryers are all produced to this module. Each one can therefore be represented by a square, 30mm by 30mm. However, for freestanding appliances – washing machines and dishwashers in particular – allow 20mm extra width so they can be manoeuvred for maintenance.

ISLAND LIFE
This is an L-shaped kitchen with an island. An island makes a very comfortable work station. It enables the cook to face the room instead of a wall. A host can chat with guests while adding finishing touches to a meal.

Arrange the cutouts in order to produce the perfect work triangle and allow space for a main work station. Start by placing the sink. The natural place is under the window for two reasons: firstly because for most of us, washing up is a bit of a chore and it is worth making it as pleasant as possible with the use of natural light; secondly because the house was probably designed with the plumbing under the window and this will make the installation easier and cheaper.

Now you can go on to deal with the cooking arrangements.

---

top tip*

If you have worktop left over in your plan consider alternative uses for it. Use a reduced width piece on the windowsill instead of ceramic tiles. Put it under an integrated washing machine to raise the height and provide a level surface or use it under a Belfast sink.

✳ Rules for Worktop Plans

✔ There must be at least 1m of space between two imaginary worktops in order to allow free movement for one person.

✔ Ideally, when a person is standing at the work surface there should be 900mm of clear space behind to provide room to bend down and open a door.

✔ If it is necessary for two people to pass at any point, such as where a traffic route crosses the work area, then the free space should be a minimum of 1.2m. Any less will create a congestion point that may lead to frayed tempers.

Hobs and Cookers

There are a number of safety requirements to meet when positioning any cooking appliance (see box below). Remembering that the kitchen should look good as well as being functional, give consideration to a strong focal point. A hob with a chimney hood above it, all in stainless steel, can be a real eye catcher, especially if centred on the wall with a balance of cabinets on each side.

SHINING EXAMPLE

The focal point here is a modern glass-and-stainless-steel cooking hood placed over an island unit hob. The result is a striking and practical solution that frees up more space for wall units.

CAUTION POSITIONING HOBS AND COOKERS

■ Ideally there should be at least 300mm of work surface each side of a cooking surface. Therefore, do not site them in a corner, at the end of a run of units or next to a sink.

■ There must be a minimum vertical distance of 650mm between the cooking surface and an extractor, and a minimum 800mm to an inflammable surface such as a cabinet. Some manufacturers may specify more so do read the installation instructions.

■ Keep them away from doors where there is an obvious danger from persons entering the room.

■ Keep them away from windows. Besides the fire risk to curtains and the possibility of a draught blowing out a pilot light, sunlight can make it difficult to distinguish if the burners are lit. This applies to ceramic and halogen hobs as well as gas.

■ Ideally, locate the cooking surface near an outside wall where steam and cooking smells can be easily extracted.

■ Do not place them below a wall-mounted boiler regardless of the separating distance.

■ Hobs must only be positioned above an oven or a base unit and not over an appliance such as a fridge or a washing machine.

■ Special rules apply to cookers with eye-level grills.

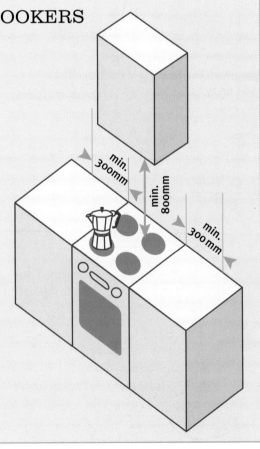

Storage Solutions

The third point of the work triangle is food storage. This will include a refrigerator, a freezer and a larder cupboard and their relative importance should be considered in that order. Obviously there are other forms of food storage such as for fresh fruit and vegetables but for the purpose of the exercise the detail can be decided later. This is the least important point of the triangle and if necessary this is where the rules can be stretched a little.

Refrigerators and Freezers

Refrigerators and freezers can be purchased in a wide variety of sizes and combinations. Some of these items are large and bulky and should not be placed in the middle of a run of units. It is better to put them at the end of a run where they will not disrupt the work surface. Most kitchen cabinet ranges include specially adapted tall units that will house an integrated fridge-freezer, giving a uniform finish (see also page 27).

Alternatively, there are individual units designed to fit under the standard worktop. A matching pair can be made to look like a single unit if placed side by side, with the door reversed on one so that they both open from the middle.

BALANCING ACT

It is best to locate tall fridge-freezers at the end of a run of units. Here, the appliance has been hidden away neatly in a special unit with doors that match the other cabinets. A tall larder unit with identical proportions, at the other end of the run, completes a symmetrical layout.

top tip*

Fridge and freezer doors must open more than 90° so that drawers and shelves can be taken out for cleaning. Take this into account if you place them in a corner.

Kitchen Units

toptip*

Locate the drawer stack close to the sink so that the top drawer can be used for cutlery.

Kitchen Units

The final task is to fit in the kitchen units and to do this it is worth spending a little time becoming familiar with the type of carcasses that are available. A look through the specification pages of a brochure may be confusing at first due to the apparent variety of shapes and sizes. However, once the units are separated into categories the job becomes more straightforward.

Standard Units

Most manufacturers keep to a format that has become the commonly accepted standard for cabinet dimensions. In order to simplify a range the standard doors are made to fit both the base (floor) and the wall units.

Generally the base and wall carcasses are sold in the same widths, as follows: 300mm, 400mm, 500mm, 600mm, 800mm, 1000mm. Cabinets up to 600mm wide will have one door (hinged on either side). The two larger sizes require two doors each.

The vertical dimensions are similar (but not identical) from one manufacturer to another. For example, a work surface height of 910mm is almost universal. This is, supposedly, a compromise between tall and short people but, in truth, is biased towards tall people. The distance between the work surface and the underside of the wall units will be about 500mm (see page 28).

Drawers

Some manufacturers still produce a range of base units with a single drawer just below the worktop (referred to as 'drawer-line'), but the usual preference is for drawers to be arranged in a stack of three or four in a 500mm or 600mm width. Some flat-pack kitchens now include deeper and wider drawers intended for pan storage.

A wide range of internal fittings made to specific drawer sizes is available. These can include cutlery dividers, pan-lid holders and even hidden ironing boards.

BREAKING UP
Making a change in the height or depth of a run of kitchen units can add visual interest.

Tall Units

Tall units are designed to span from the bottom of the base units to the top of the wall units. They are available in 300mm, 500mm and 600mm widths. All three widths come as larder or broom cupboards but the 600mm units are made to incorporate integrated appliances such as ovens and combination fridge/freezers. Some care must be taken when specifying these units because they may be specific to particular appliances.

toptip*

Always site tall units at the end of a run of units and never in the middle. Wall units should be fitted above base units and not on their own so that people do not bump their heads.

DIVIDE AND RULE

Drawers are the ideal storage space for the many small items that accumulate in a kitchen. Flexible internal storage fittings provide a place for everything – so no more rummaging through the clutter for a hidden teaspoon.

NEAT CORNERING

An efficient way of utilizing the space in an L-shaped corner unit is to fit carousel shelves such as these.

Corner Units

The most common corner base unit is a 1000mm carcass with a 500mm door which must be set 100mm from the return wall so that the door is clear of the 600mm wide worktop. Some manufacturers produce a more versatile unit with a 400mm door designed to fit tight into the corner or a unit with a 600mm door that is fitted 200mm from the return wall. Another way of dealing with a corner is to use an L-shaped unit which has an equal return on each side. The backs of these units are usually 2 x 900mm (but some are 925mm each side). The fronts will have two 300mm doors hinged together.

Similarly, different manufacturers have different solutions for corner wall cabinets. The vertical lines should match up with the base units. One solution is a 600mm unit with a single door at 45°. A less common solution is similar to the 1000mm corner base unit where the run of units on the return wall butts up to a blanking panel.

Anatomy of **Kitchen Wall and Base Unit Carcasses**

The profile of the units illustrated below represents a typical middle-range kitchen. They have one adjustable shelf and the doors (not shown) fit both the wall and the base units. Between the back panel and the wall there is a void space for running services.

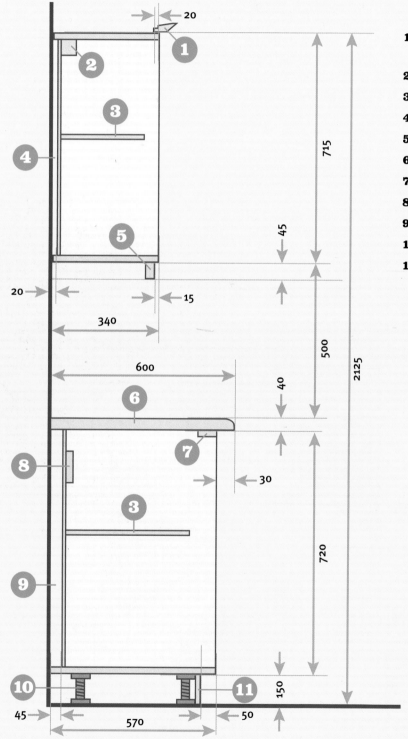

1 Cornice (overlaps wall cabinet top by about 20mm)

2 Wall fixing inside the cabinet

3 Adjustable shelf

4 Void (20mm)

5 Pelmet

6 Work surface (600mm wide)

7 Front rail

8 Back rail

9 Service void (45mm)

10 Adjustable-height legs

11 Plinth (about 150mm high)

Display Units

Display units are either completely open or have glazed doors. Because the interior will be visible the carcass is finished to match the door colour. Open-ended base and wall units may be available that are designed to go at the end of a run of units.

A stylish display unit is the dresser. This sits on the worktop with the top of the unit level with the top of the wall units. The standard dresser has one glazed door and two cute mini drawers at the bottom. They are very effective when a low voltage light is installed at the top and glass shelves are used to replace those supplied.

CLEVER COMBINATIONS
If you have a lot of recipe books, it would be worth incorporating open shelves into your kitchen design *(top right)*. The colourful display unit *(below right)* and the more traditional dresser *(below)* are stylish storage solutions.

Guildelines for Positioning Kitchen Units

✔ There is always a potential problem of wasted space at the corners so it is best to begin by sorting out corner solutions.

✔ Usually, match the wall units to the base units (see above). Ideally, a 500mm door on a base unit should be replicated by a 500mm door on the wall unit above, both with handles on the same side.

✔ The exception to the above is when working from a focal point such as a hob or cooker with a chimney hood above. In this situation it may be necessary to place the wall units first and then work back.

✔ It is not sensible to try and use every centimetre of space. When you come to fitting the kitchen you may come to regret a tight design. Small gaps will allow for discrepancies and distortions and can be sorted out using fillers (see page 98).

✔ A small gap of 150mm to 300mm could be filled with a wine rack, towel rail or narrow cabinet (see below left).

✔ Never arrange wall units tight into a corner if you intend to tile the walls. This could restrict the tile layout or prevent the doors from opening.

✔ The smallest unit that will house a single bowl sink is 500mm wide. A 1$\frac{1}{2}$ bowl sink will require a unit at least 600mm wide.

✔ When working along from an internal corner allow at least 40mm space for the door handle. This is particularly important when an appliance with a drop-down door, such as a dishwasher, is sited next to a standard corner unit.

✔ Sinks and hobs have to be cut into the worktop. Keep them well away from worktop joints to avoid creating a weak spot (see diagram below).

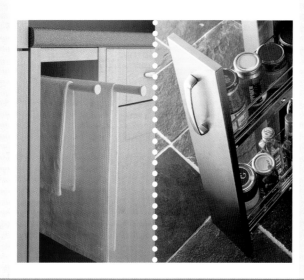

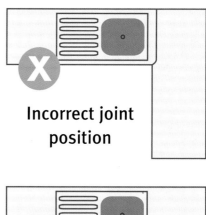

Incorrect joint position

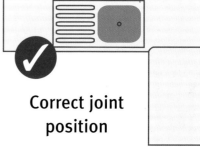

Correct joint position

ROLL UP

A stylish innovation is a roller slide-down front similar to those seen on old-fashioned roll-top desks, called tambour units *(right)*. They are popular with interior designers when a minimalist look is required. Toasters, kettles, coffee makers and other small appliances, can be neatly tucked away simply by pulling down the shutter. Tambour units are often fitted with socket outlets so that the wires are hidden away too.

End Panels and Trims

End panels and trims are colour coordinated to match the chosen door and drawer fronts. End panels are often used to cover the exposed end of a run of units and mask the standard carcass colour. Sometimes replacement gables are available for this purpose but often the only solution is a panel cut to fit. These panels may also be required to support the worktop, such as at the side of an appliance. In this case they may be referred to as end support panels or ESPs.

Trims refer to three items: cornice, pelmet and plinth. The cornice is fitted to the top of the wall units and tall units. The pelmet runs round the bottom of the wall units and is used to conceal any under-unit lighting. The cornice and pelmet help strengthen the wall units but the main purpose is to link the units and make them look like one piece of furniture. The plinth or kick-board fills the space between the bottom of the carcasses and the floor. Trims are supplied in standard lengths of 2.4m or 3m, and have to be cut to fit.

KEEPING TRIM

A cornice *(top)* has been added to link the wall units and unify the separate components. The pelmet *(bottom)*, conceals the under-unit lighting, creating a neat, professional finish. Both trims help to strengthen the units.

top tip*

Remember that the necessity for a support panel beside an appliance will increase the length of the run by the thickness of the panel.

do it ADD KITCHEN UNITS TO THE ROOM PLAN

In addition to the work triangle (see below), take account of the need for a main work station and the direction of flow. The plans illustrated here are working layouts for the Case Study kitchen on page 50.

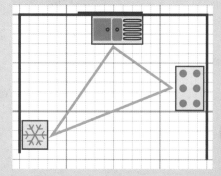

1 The sink is commonly located in the centre of a window **A** but it could be moved up to 500mm to either side to accommodate the base units.

2 Locate the cooking area **B**. Decide on the type of appliance: an under-counter oven with a hob over; a split-level oven in a tall housing and separate hob; or a range cooker. If the second option is chosen the oven housing has to go at the end of a run.

3 Choose an approximate position for the fridge/freezer **C**. A tall version should be at the end of a run.

4 Choose base units for the corners **D**. This kitchen uses both types.

5 Locate wet appliances **E**. The choices may be restricted by the hot and cold water supply and the waste. If the waste has to go into a SSP (usually in the corner of the room) there must be a clear path to run the waste pipe. Some provision may have to be made to fit a standpipe, such as in a void beside the machine or behind the units.

6 Adjust the gaps to suit standard kitchen unit sizes. For instance, a 600mm gap = 600mm unit or 2 x 300mm units.

7 Finally, address style considerations.

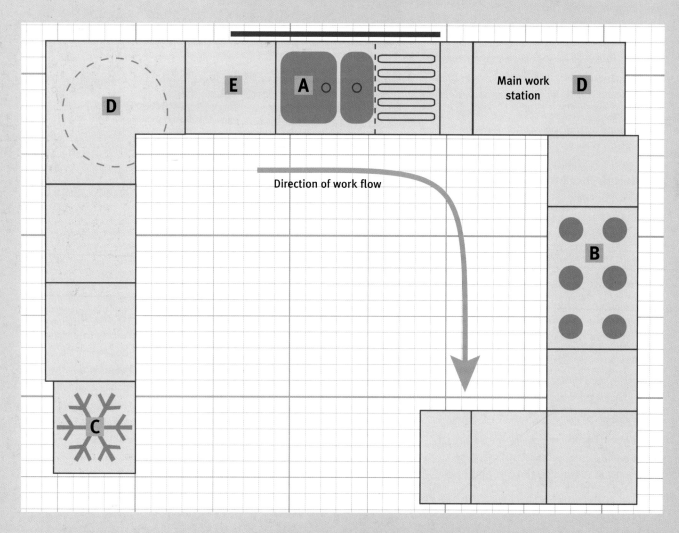

Size Isn't Everything: Planning a Small Kitchen

Contrary to the images displayed in glossy magazines, most kitchens are small with only a dozen or fewer units. Many of us live in flats converted from larger properties and the kitchen is often squeezed into an awkward shape. When working with a narrow or irregular space, it is especially important to make the best use of what is available. Here are some ideas to help you plan a kitchen that is small but perfectly formed.

(right) If your kitchen has high ceilings, make the most of this space by stacking two rows of wall cabinets on top of each other. You may have to stand on something to reach things down from the top shelves, so use these to store things you only need occasionally.

For narrow spaces consider the use of smaller doors. A 600mm cabinet with two 300mm doors will be less obtrusive than the standard 600mm door.

Look out for ingenious storage solutions such as plinth drawers.

(above) Maximize the use of corner base units by fitting accessories such as carousel shelves or a magic corner.

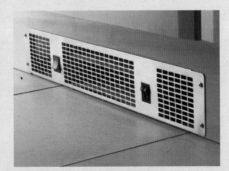

(left) Utilize the space between the work surface and wall cabinets with clever storage systems to keep everyday items at hand.

If the room is not wide enough for a standard 600mm wide worktop at each side then install wall units instead of base units and reduce the worktop on top to a width of 400mm. Alternatively, fit standard units down one side only but fit a 700mm worktop to compensate and create a generous work station. Or consider stacking wall units one on top of another, separated with a cut down section of worktop to maintain the line.

(above) Create more wall space by removing an awkward radiator. Heat the room using underfloor heating or a kickspace heater instead.

Freestanding refrigerators, freezers and cookers are available in widths of 500mm. These are worth considering if space is tight.

Choosing a Style

CITY SLICKER
A stylish, contemporary kitchen is perfect in the context of a city centre apartment. With its modern combination of glossy black worktops and warm wood units, it will also appeal to prospective buyers of the property.

Style is the result of presenting things in a pleasing way. We can identify and make use of the distinctive qualities that characterize a particular style: the elegant proportions of Georgian architecture for example, or the warmth of an English country farmhouse. We can look to past or present, town or country. We can take ideas from a particular school of thought, gain inspiration from an individual, or draw ideas from cultures around the world. There is a vast repertoire of sources on which to base a choice for your kitchen.

Source Material

Start with the architecture of your home. The kitchen should look as if it belongs to the house. A strong farmhouse design may jar the senses when set in a modern apartment but a country style would be perfectly at home in a cottage. Look for style clues in the age of the building: the kitchen does not have to be authentic to the time when the house was built but the era will have its own style characteristics which can be reinterpreted and modified.

In the context of your home the kitchen is rarely in isolation because people move about the house. There should be design links between adjacent rooms allowing the decor of one to merge with the other. Fundamentally, basic joinery should be the same, at least on each floor. Doors, architraves and skirting should match and make each room feel part of the whole. But the idea of links can be extended to style features such as colour and materials that should lead from one room to another without shocking the senses.

The worst mistake is to rush into a decision. Visit the showrooms of kitchen retailers to collect ideas. Cut out pictures of kitchens that appeal from magazines and brochures. Browse the internet and print out colour images of things that catch the eye. Gradually put together a source of reference material. After a while, go through the collection and try to sort it into 'must haves', possibilities and 'not-any-more' piles. Eventually a style will emerge.

Popular Styles

Styles are subject to fashion and are constantly evolving. Once you've plumped for a style that suits you try to incorporate it into every detail to make the most impact. Keep your chosen style in mind when sourcing paint colours, lighting, cupboard handles and tiles, for example.

Some of the most popular styles are described here, together with suggestions on how to create the look for each. On pages 14 and 50 you'll find detailed case studies of two very different kitchens that might help to inspire you.

top tip*

If you're not planning to stay in your home long term, bear in mind that the kitchen style you choose could put off a prospective future buyer of your property. Sticking to a simple classic or contemporary style is the best option and you can still stamp your own mark on it in the accessories.

Minimalist

The key features of minimalism are clean lines and a complete absence of clutter. Small appliances (kettle, toaster) are hidden away, perhaps in a tambour unit (see page 31). Choose blinds instead of curtains or leave windows exposed. Walls will often be plain white, so this clinical look can benefit from the introduction of one bright colour. A simple vase with a striking, single flower will set off the design.

Farmhouse

The warmth and comfort of rustic simplicity is the goal. Use natural timber for worktops, such as beech block or maple, to set off a ceramic sink. Consider leaded light doors and wrought iron handles. Where finances allow, feature a traditional range cooker or an Aga set in an opened-up chimneybreast. Finish the chimney with a robust wooden shelf on ornate brackets on which to display earthenware dishes. When space permits, have a central table of generous proportions. Use hardwearing natural materials such as terracotta and stone – exposed brickwork works well.

Hi-tech

This style draws inspiration from commercial kitchens. It is an industrial look, with rugged, ultra-hygienic, uncluttered spaces with a feeling of efficiency. Brushed stainless steel is mandatory. Look out for range cookers made by manufacturers normally associated with commercial catering equipment. Choose practical, chunky metal handles. A strong vibrant colour will complement the stainless steel.

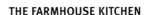

THE FARMHOUSE KITCHEN
This traditional kitchen features warm wood, terracotta and white-painted units, offset by a dramatic teal blue. The wall panelling and Aga surround are painted the same colour as the units, pulling the whole scheme together.

COUNTRY COOKING
Antique and reclaimed pieces will enhance a period kitchen *(above)*. A suspended rack, displaying copper pans, dried herbs and garlic, is a striking feature.

Country

Country kitchen units are often painted in pale colours, particularly cream. Dresser units with glass doors look good – bridge the space between two dressers with open shelves on which to display everyday china. Pull-out wicker baskets are an ideal country storage solution. Use tongue-and-groove panelling between worktops and wall units in the same colour as the doors. Hardwood work surfaces and draining boards, combined with a Belfast sink and traditional taps, complete the country look.

Shaker

The Shakers did not believe in uneccessary decoration; their style was understated and uncluttered, with an emphasis on clean, simple lines. Woodwork should be pale and natural. Introduce colour with muted reds or blues. A typical feature is a peg rail fixed around the room at head height.

Georgian

The Georgian period is associated with elegant simplicity. Style was heavily influenced by the architecture of ancient Greece and Rome, with proportion, order and symmetry being the key features. Common colours were subdued: pearl, lead, faded rose pink and natural stone colours were all popular. Simple painted units will work well or look for bleached oak. Avoid embellishments and choose large wooden knobs or brass D-handles on drawers. If you have sufficient space consider a section of floor-to-ceiling cabinets made out of stacked wall units and a plain and simple central table. Look for a fireclay sink with piecrust edges. Copper and brass are suitable, but don't use stainless steel.

toptip*

In a period kitchen, try to find a suitable spot to feature a reclaimed piece. It can be tremendous fun trawling auctions and reclamation yards to find suitable items. An old butcher's block or a small church pew can work well but if you have sufficient space hunt out a genuine pine dresser or a house-keeper's cupboard. The shabby elegance that such pieces exude can be just the thing to give the kitchen character and personality. Even in small kitchens such items as an old shop sign can be used to enhance the period look.

GEORGIAN ELEGANCE

Be inspired by classic proportions *(above)*. The design of the cabinet doors echoes the shape of the shutters and fireplace. The walls have been painted a muted green, typical of the Georgian period, that perfectly complements the oak cabinets and limestone floor.

toptip*

Several paint manufacturers (see page 170) produce their own versions of period paints that are suited to Georgian, Victorian and early twentieth-century interiors.

Victorian

The Victorian kitchen is less restrained than Georgian style. During this period brighter colours became available, and pattern and decoration were popular. Kitchen units should reflect this. They should have more ornamentation than the restrained architectural look of a Georgian kitchen. For example, the cornice can be more elaborate and glass doors on Gothic-style display units would be appropriate. Use lots of tiling and consider including a decorative frieze.

Contemporary

This is a cool, restful and clean look with a Scandinavian influence. Use pale wood with minimal graining such as maple or birch. Set it off with brushed metal handles, taps and light fittings (aluminium or nickel). Contrast striking modern accessories with natural materials: leather, linen and silk. Laminated wood floors suit this look. Colours should be modern and fresh.

CONTEMPORARY STYLE

If you don't want a traditional kitchen or an ultra-trendy one, the simple, modern approach *(above)* will suit most properties and should appeal to a wide range of prospective buyers.

Borrowing from the Past: a Traditional Family Kitchen

Whatever your tastes, it is likely that your choice of kitchen will fall into one of two categories: traditional or modern. Your taste and the type of property will govern your final choice but consider, too, the practical aspects of the style of kitchen. A family kitchen should be practical and hardwearing, to withstand all the knocks of family life, but it can be stylish, too. The traditional approach easily accommodates these key requirements.

The wood work surface above the drawer unit adds an extra texture.

An inset ceramic sink and pewter mixer tap combine traditional style with modern convenience.

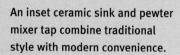

Open shelving means everyday objects are kept close to hand and is a great display place for the family's favourite belongings.

Apothecary-style drawers are both stylish and a very practical choice for storage.

Ivory painted cupboard doors and units are ideal for the traditional look of a farmhouse kitchen. Pewter door knobs, in an antique design, turn modern flatpack units into pieces of classic furniture.

The rich, warm colours of this granite provide an attractive and practical (if rather expensive) work surface that will last for years. It would need to be cut and fitted professionally.

A Modern Hi-tech Kitchen for the Urban Home

Shiny, white units and stainless steel may not be the right choice for a family kitchen (it would show up grubby marks in no time), but this style is perfect for the urban professional who wants the wow-factor.

The open-plan layout is geared up for sociable cooking. With plenty of storage to hide away the clutter and the effective use of task lighting, the result is a stylish, yet incredibly practical kitchen.

High-gloss white doors and drawers reflect the light in this small kitchen area which receives little natural daylight. The chunky but minimally styled chrome handles also have a high-polish finish.

The latest hi-tech chimney-style extractor hood, in sleek stainless steel, is essential for this look.

The steel theme is continued in the details, including a splashback of easy to clean steel tiles.

An area of wenge timber work surface separates the kitchen from the living space in this open-plan, loft-style apartment. The dark wood provides a contrast to all the shiny steel used elsewhere, and prevents an overly clinical feel.

A stainless steel work surface is what every serious modern chef wants. This one extends almost seamlessly into a smooth double sink.

'Gadget' accessories are another feature in the modern minimalist kitchen. Here, the humble mixer tap is given the twenty-first century treatment with a flexible handspray hose.

✳ Some Interior Design Tricks

will enhance the other and create visually interesting effects. Contemporary black kitchen units *(below left)* are enhanced by the contrast with stainless steel doors and accessories.

✔ Colour influences our emotions. Cool colours *(above top)* produce a calm, relaxed atmosphere, whereas warm colours *(above bottom)* are welcoming and stimulating.

✔ Strong tones, warm colours *(above)* and distinctive patterns advance, making walls appear closer. Use them on the end walls of long narrow rooms.

✔ By contrast, cool colours and pale tones recede, making them useful for small rooms.

✔ Contrasts can produce aesthetically pleasing results. Consider combining natural with synthetic, old with new, cold with warm, rough with shiny, or hard with soft textures. Often one

✔ Light-coloured natural wood cabinets *(below)* can tend to brighten and sometimes enlarge a space.

✔ Use warm natural materials – brick, wood, granite and natural fibres – for a cosy, friendly and relaxed feel *(above)*.

✔ Use off-whites in preference to stark white for a more expensive look.

✔ Cold materials are hard and smooth: gloss paint, polished granite, stainless steel *(below)*. Use them to produce a contemporary feel.

✔ Diagonal patterns (chevrons) give the illusion of width. Diagonal tiling on floors or walls will help to create space.

✔ Oblong tiles arranged in a brickwork pattern *(above)* will make a wall look longer.

✔ Glass promotes an impression of space. Make the most of windows and put glass panels in doors.

✔ The lines created in tongue-and-groove panelling will make a room seem taller.

✔ In small kitchens keep the design plain and simple. Use pale, natural colours. Avoid fussy details and obvious pattern. Make a concerted effort to keep clutter to a minimum. Integrated appliances *(below)* will help to keep clean lines.

Lighting

LET THE LIGHT IN
Even if the windows in your kitchen aren't as big as these, you can still create a bright and airy feel by making the most of natural light. Any window treatments should be unobtusive; try using pale colours to bounce the light around the room.

top tip*

For the latest ideas in lighting look at the ways in which designers use electrical lights in high-street shops.

To create a safe and hygienic environment good light is essential and this should be taken into consideration at the planning stage. Natural light is best. It is the most restful to work in and does not distort the colour of food. Therefore, before thinking of artificial lighting, consider how to make good use of the natural daylight. Is it possible to enlarge a window without compromising the kitchen layout? Perhaps a window could convert to a pair of French doors? If the kitchen is in a single storey it may be possible to put a skylight in the roof, or if the roof is flat, then a lantern ceiling could be very effective.

Artificial lighting enables the light to be manipulated to better effect. As technology advances, so the possibilities grow. To understand how to use lighting in the home think of it as serving three different functions: general lighting, task lighting and decorative lighting.

General Lighting

This is the system that is normally reached for when moving about the house. The switch will be located just inside the door and this provides the overall lighting with no concentration. In the past, general lighting was characterized by a central light pendant and in the kitchen this would have become a fluorescent fitting in order to provide a brighter working light.

The introduction of 12-volt tungsten halogen bulbs has enabled the light source to be hidden away in the ceiling void. When they are dotted about they can produce a consistent general light. In today's multifunctional kitchen they are particularly useful. If separate circuits, controlled by dimmer switches, are installed above the various zones, the emphasis can be adjusted according to the use of the room. Just like a theatre, the lights can be made to follow the action.

✳ Rules for 12-volt Lights

✔ To calculate the number of lights required consider the central area of the room to be 0.5m in from the walls. As a quick guide, allow 1 x 20w wide-angle beam light per square metre or 1 x 50w wide beam per 1.5 square metres.

✔ To maximize bulb life, try to match the transformer output to the total wattage of the bulbs.

✔ The same regulations apply to 12v systems as 230v systems. Despite the low voltage, cables should be joined using junction boxes, *not* with connection blocks and electrical tape. Mark the junction box with a felt tip pen as '12v'.

✔ Replace blown bulbs as soon as possible. Delay will cause 'over-volting' of the other bulbs and reduce their lifespan.

✔ When cabinet lights are supplied from the ring main a 3A fuse must be inserted in the plug or FCU.

✔ Tungsten halogen bulbs dissipate 60% of their heat from the rear. When they are installed in an enclosed space clear away any thermal insulation and protect nearby timber.

✔ Do not connect 12v systems to the 'earth'.

✔ Control lights with a switch on the mains voltage side of the transformer.

Task Lighting

General lighting will need to be enhanced when it is inadequate for performing tasks such as food preparation and washing up. Furthermore, the work stations in kitchens are usually around the edge of the room and this can mean working in one's own shadow if the main source of light is from behind. To avoid this situation, consider ways to bring light onto the work area. The usual method is to install lights below the wall units but a smart effect can be achieved by putting them above the units; either as stalk-lights or recessed into a flyover.

Decorative Lighting

By its very nature, light will direct the eye and can therefore be very effective in defining a decorative style. Self-illuminated glass shelves enhance a hi-tech look. A focused spotlight can be made to pick out a specific feature, such as a flower display. A couple of pendant lights hanging over a table can create a strong statement. Even a simple low voltage spotlight inside a display unit can be used to great effect.

TASK FORCE
Recessed spotlights, either in the ceiling *(top left)* or under a shelf or unit *(top right)* are stylish and unobtrusive. The traditional pendant lamps *(bottom right)* are suitable for a period kitchen and the modern stalk lights *(bottom left)* are an unusual way of incorporating task lighting above the wall units.

Kitchen Services

PLAN AHEAD
Details such as lighting inside wall cabinets can add much to the appeal and efficiency of your kitchen, but it is vital to consider them at the planning stage.

When restyling an existing kitchen, time and money will be saved if the appliances are located in the same place as they were before. Unfortunately, this may restrict planning freedom when, for the sake of avoiding a little inconvenience, so much more could be possible. The guidelines below will help you plan the location of electric points.

CAUTION ELECTRIC SAFETY

■ Any alterations to the kitchen circuits must comply with the latest regulations. See page 155.
■ If there is an electric point, such as a socket or a switch, within 800mm of the tap it must be moved.

■ Electric points should be at least 150mm horizontally away from a hob.
■ Plug sockets should be a minimum of 450mm and a maximum of 1200mm from the floor. The centre of a plug socket must be at least 150mm above a worktop.

■ Surface-mounted plug sockets can be installed high up in base units where they will not be obstructed by the cabinet contents. They can be incorporated into an extension of the ring main or as a spur (see also page 164).
■ If the supply to an appliance cannot be installed in an adjacent cabinet consider extending its cable.
■ The alternative to a plug socket is an FCU (Fused Connection Unit). These incorporate a cartridge fuse, and can have an on/off switch. From the outlet (or load), a cable can be run to the wall behind the appliance and terminated in a cable-outlet plate. They can be installed on the wall above the worktop to control an appliance below.
■ If the connection is made behind an integrated appliance there must be an additional isolation point in an accessible position. Use an FCU.
■ Consider a cabinet light system as another appliance. Power can be provided from a plug socket or an FCU (see *Anatomy of a Simple 12v Lighting System*, page 46).

min. 150mm
min. 150mm
min. 150mm
min. 800mm
min. 800mm

✳ Positioning Plumbing Services

✔ If kitchen waste water must be piped into the SSP (soil stack pipe) it may restrict the possible location of the sink to one or other of the adjacent walls.

✔ The stopcock is used to isolate domestic plumbing from the mains and is frequently located in the kitchen; usually under the sink for convenience. It is vital that the new arrangement enables easy access in an emergency. If you intend to move the position of the sink the stopcock may have to be relocated or, when this is beyond DIY competence, a second stopcock could be installed on an extension of the incoming water supply.

✔ When the original stopcock is left in place be aware that it may impede whatever is intended to sit over it. If it is to be a cabinet then a cutout at the back could get over the problem. However, if an appliance is planned in this position the stopcock may have to be relocated.

✔ Dishwashers in particular leave very little clearance. They need the full depth to the wall and will only enable the standard hot and cold pipes to run behind if they are kept within 150mm of the floor. One solution is to fit a wider worktop. This will enable the carcasses to be brought forward and leave a wider service void behind.

✔ Wider worktops are also the solution for inconvenient waste pipes and can be used to accommodate the standpipe for a wet appliance when it is located away from the sink.

✔ Door openings present an obstacle for pipe runs. If the kitchen has a suspended floor the hot and cold water pipes can be re-routed underneath. With solid floors there may be no other alternative but to cut out a channel in the screed.

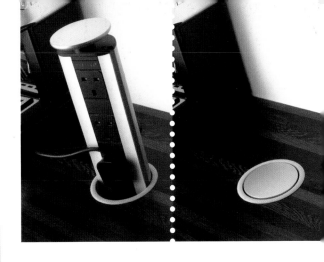

MORE POWER
You may well have more electrical appliances than the original owner of your kitchen. This retractable socket strip *(above)* provides extra outlets when they are needed and, when not in use, is concealed under the surface. It also avoids the need to channel out walls for wiring.

Making an Electrical Installation Plan

Fitting a new kitchen provides a rare opportunity to upgrade the electrical installation. New plug sockets can be put in to suit the way the kitchen will be used. Any that have become redundant or are in dangerous positions can be taken out. If your kitchen has a huge, old-fashioned cooker control, this is the time to replace it with a neat 45A switch no bigger than a single plug socket.

For the sake of clear communication, take a spare copy of the final plan and mark it up with the changes to be made (see *Plan Symbols* on page 19). The plan should also show the position of each appliance so that the arrangement for the power supply can be decided. The modern trend is to de-clutter the wall surface and 'hide' the connections inside the base units. This arrangement is perfectly acceptable providing each appliance has an accessible isolation switch or plug-socket.

Anatomy of a **Simple 12v Lighting System**

The system illustrated can be installed by a
non-qualified DIY electrician because it does
not interfere with a fixed wiring circuit.

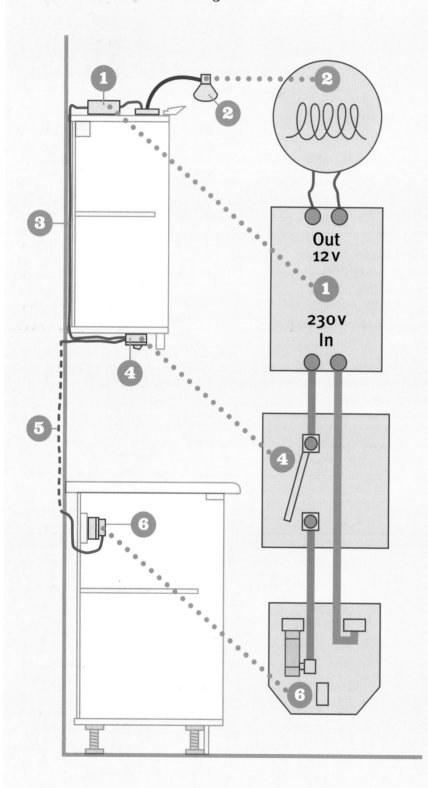

1 230v/12v transformer

2 12v halogen light (probably
   one of three)

3 Cable in void

4 Switch

5 Cable chased into wall

6 3-pin plug (with 3amp fuse)

The power is supplied from a plug
fitted with a 3amp fuse. A flexible
0.75mm twin cable is run into the
service void at the back of the base
unit and chased up the wall (see
page 75 B) to the bottom of the wall
unit where it is taken to the switch.
The 'live' brown cable is cut and
connected to the two terminals of
the switch before the cable is taken
through the service void of the wall
unit to be connected to the input
(230v) terminals of the transformer.
Connect the 12v lights to the output
(12v) terminals. If tube lights are
used instead, take the cable from the
switch to the first light and then link
any others one by one.

Firming up Your Plan

Now that you have a final kitchen plan you can make a list of all the things that you will need to purchase and order. Attention to detail at this stage will pay dividends later on, so remember to include all the small items such as rawl plugs, stretcher plates and screws that would hold you up if they were not available when you most need them.

Thorough planning is crucial to the success of your kitchen fit. Not only will the work proceed more quickly but also it is much easier to sort out problems on paper rather than when all around is in chaos. An incorrect measurement could lead to serious problems during the fitting stage so check and double check.

The plan shown on the right is a working layout for the Case Study kitchen on pages 166-167.

Run through the *Planning Checklist* below before you firm up your final plan.

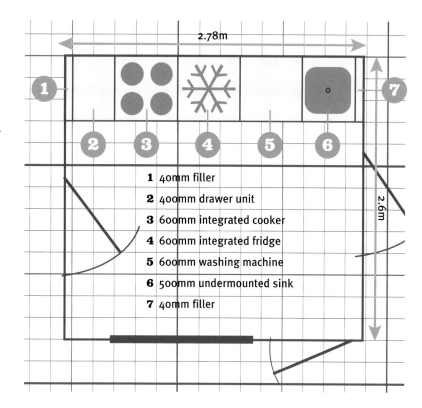

2.78m

2.6m

1 40mm filler
2 400mm drawer unit
3 600mm integrated cooker
4 600mm integrated fridge
5 600mm washing machine
6 500mm undermounted sink
7 40mm filler

✳ Planning Checklist

✔ **ASSESS PRESENT AND FUTURE NEEDS**
changing lifestyle; aging/growing family

✔ **CONSIDER THE MERITS AND PITFALLS OF THE EXISTING KITCHEN**
efficiency, safety, hygiene

✔ **ASSESS FEASIBILITY OF BUILDING ALTERATIONS**
check adjacent rooms; exterior space to extend; the potential to swap over to another room

✔ **MAKE A PRELIMINARY BUDGET**
how much is it worth spending; how much can you afford?

✔ **DRAW A SCALE PLAN**

✔ **COLLECT POTENTIAL EXAMPLES**
magazines; brochures; visit showrooms

✔ **DECIDE ON THE STYLE**

✔ **FINALIZE LAYOUT**

✔ **DECIDE ON QUALITY OF DIFFERENT ELEMENTS**

✔ **ASSESS YOUR OWN SKILLS**
what jobs can you tackle?
do you have a family member or friend with skills?

✔ **HARDEN UP ON BUDGET**

✔ **ORGANIZE FINANCE**

✔ **MAKE APPLICATION TO LOCAL AUTHORITY**

✔ **CHECK DIARY FOR SUITABLE PERIOD**

✔ **PLACE ORDERS AND AGREE DELIVERY DATES**

Options for the Worktop Surface

7

LAMINATE Readily available and inexpensive, with a huge variety of designs. Laminate needs sympathetic use because although it is reasonably tough, it will scratch and some liquids can stain. Once damaged it cannot be repaired.

HARDWOOD A natural, attractive and tactile surface. Its appearance will change with age; some say it becomes more attractive as the timber seasons and the patination develops. It is important to regularly apply a drying oil such as Danish oil to maintain a water-repellent surface. Scratches can be rubbed out with fine sandpaper.

GRANITE Luxurious and immensely hardwearing, but expensive. Under normal conditions it will not scratch and hot pans will not burn the surface. It comes in many colour and grain pattern variations. Most granite is porous and requires sealing. It has to be cut and prepared in a dedicated workshop and is generally not suitable for DIY.

MARBLE Polished marble has a similar appeal to granite. However, it is a much softer stone that will scratch and stain. It is therefore unsuitable where appearance is important.

COMPOSITE STONE Several proprietary versions are made from crushed quartz and silicates mixed with resin, colour and binders. It has the same qualities as granite, without being brittle and absorbent, and is of similar price.

CORIAN Manufactured using powder and resin. It can be moulded to virtually any shape so that a worktop can incorporate a sink in a seamless finish. Corian is prized for its hygienic qualities, but it is even more expensive than granite.

STAINLESS STEEL Impervious, hardwearing and heatproof. Its stylish good looks soon dull with use; use baby oil to revitalise the surface. It can be shaped to any surface and sinks and drainers can be fully integrated into worktops.

do it PLAN THE WORKTOP LAYOUT

It will be useful to make up a simple sketch plan of the worktop layout to indicate the intended cutting arrangement. At each corner there are two choices; one worktop will run to the wall and have a female cut along the front edge, the other worktop butts onto this and has a male cut. For the worktop with the male cut add at least another 100mm to the length to

assist the router jig **A**. Remember to keep any joints away from cutouts required for the sink or the hob. Special bolts are used to clamp worktop joints together (page 93). They are let into the underside of the worktop and need at least 80mm each side of the join. If the join is too close to a cutout then a serious weak spot will be created.

If the kitchen is U-shaped try to avoid having one length of worktop at the bottom of the U that fits from wall to wall **B**. This will lead to fitting difficulties later on.

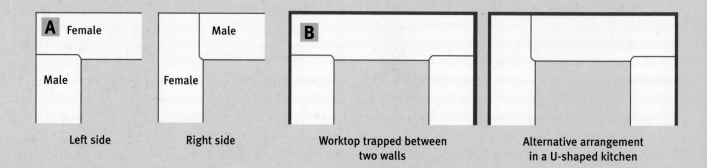

A Female	Male
Male	Female
Left side	Right side

B Worktop trapped between two walls

Alternative arrangement in a U-shaped kitchen

MAKE A FINAL KITCHEN SHOPPING LIST

Kitchen Units

Mark each unit on your plan with a number that will correspond to a list. Against the number on the list identify each unit with a short description such as '500 wall unit, glazed door'. Ideally, add the manufacturer's code number to avoid confusion.

Gables and Decor Panels

Where add-on or replacement gables are required mark them on the plan with a highlighter. Remember to mark any ESPs and the back panel for a breakfast bar. Count up the number required for each type and add them to your list.

Plinth

If the kitchen style requires add-on gables that go down to the floor it will not be necessary to allow for 'returns' because the plinth will butt up to the gables. Measure the distance along each run of units and on inside corners allow for an overlap. One length of plinth will need to run under the carcass to connect with a hidden leg. The plinth on the adjoining run will butt up to this but because the plinth is set back from the front of the unit allow for an extra 100mm.

Cornice

Measure the length of each unit face and at each corner add another 100mm to account for the mitre. For example, a 1000mm wall unit on its own would require a front piece 1000mm long plus 2 x 100mm for each corner. The two exposed sides would require 2 x 340mm plus 2 x 100mm. The total length required would be at least 2080mm. Don't over-economize.

Pelmet

All that is necessary is to measure the length of the front edges and add on the returns at the end of each run. Convert this into lengths of pelmet.

Fillers

The fillers have to be cut on site from ESPs, plinth or spare gables. Identify them on the plan and decide what they will be produced from. Adjust the quantity accordingly.

Cabinet Doors

The specification for each unit will include the doors/drawers. However, when integrated appliances are being used their doors must be added to the order.

Worktops

If you intend using laminate worktops, consider the position of the joint because this may affect the number of lengths required (see page 48).

Sink and Taps

Some sinks can only be fitted one way round: with the draining board on the right or the left. Don't forget to include the waste fittings (waste outlet, overflow and plug) which must be matched to the design of the sink. Check the tap to see how it connects to the water supply pipes. Some European taps have 10mm tail pipes and to connect them to the 15mm supply pipes will require two 15/10mm reducing couplers (either compression or push fit).

Plumbing Supplies

The trap: the most versatile is a P-trap with a telescopic extension. If the washing machine and/or the dishwasher is to be located close to the sink, order a trap with one or two spigot inlets that enable the waste hose from the machine to be connected to the trap. If either of these wet appliances is too far from the sink use a similar P-trap with a length of 40mm pipe to make up a stand pipe. For the waste: order at least one 3m length of 40mm diameter solvent weld pipe together with various solvent weld fittings dependent on the course that the pipe must travel. Remember a pot of solvent weld adhesive and pipe clips.

Electrical Supplies

Revamping a kitchen provides an opportunity to upgrade the sockets and other electrical accessories. Sockets and switches are available in a variety of finishes such as stainless steel and enamel. You may find a modern equivalent that enhances the style of the room.

Accessories

Some items may not come as standard and as a consequence have to be ordered. For example, each worktop joint will require at least two toggle bolts (see page 118). If the worktop abuts a freestanding cooker, the ends must be finished with aluminium end caps. Consider other accessories such as: handles, breakfast bar legs, cutlery trays, waste bins, pull-out towel rails, extra shelves, carousel units, magic corners, soft closers, edging strip and various types of pull-out baskets.

Lighting

The task lights that fit under wall units can be either fluorescent tube or low voltage. If you opt for tube lights look out for the ultra-slim type that incorporate a triphosphor tube. Up to ten units can be linked together. Low voltage lighting must be matched to a transformer. A 20–60VA electronic transformer can power up to three 20W lamps. They can be mounted in very decorative fittings for mounting above or below the wall units.

Case Study 2: a Kitchen in a New Extension to a Cottage

The owners wanted to build an extension to include a bigger kitchen and breakfast room and convert the existing kitchen area into a dining room. The fundamental plan for the kitchen was drawn up first and the structure of the extension was planned around it. The owners were to hold regular dinner parties for up to eight people in the dining room adjacent to the new kitchen. Informal meals, however, could be taken in an area put aside in the new extension. Therefore the kitchen layout had to enable a flow in two directions and also to incorporate plenty of storage and work surfaces.

The kitchen needed to reflect the owner's busy lifestyle and so a lot of thought was given to a labour-saving arrangement with a perfect work triangle. She is right-handed and therefore the natural way for her to work is in a clockwise direction. The flow from storage to sink to cooker to service was worked out in reverse, working backwards from the dining room. A U-shaped

arrangement has been designed, with a small peninsular outside the dining room door to act as a serving station/collection point. The peninsular will also serve as a barrier to keep guests away from the cooking area. The sink is placed on an outside wall to make the most of natural daylight.

The main storage area, opposite the range cooker, another peninsular formed of wall units placed back to back with base units. This serves to screen off the kitchen from the secondary dining area. It is the natural place for the kettle, the toaster and the microwave.

The style needs to blend in but not be too 'country cottage'. As it is on view when entertaining it will have to be smart. Natural oak units in a simple style are unlikely to date. Granite worktops complement them perfectly, providing a durable, labour-saving surface with a luxurious appeal.

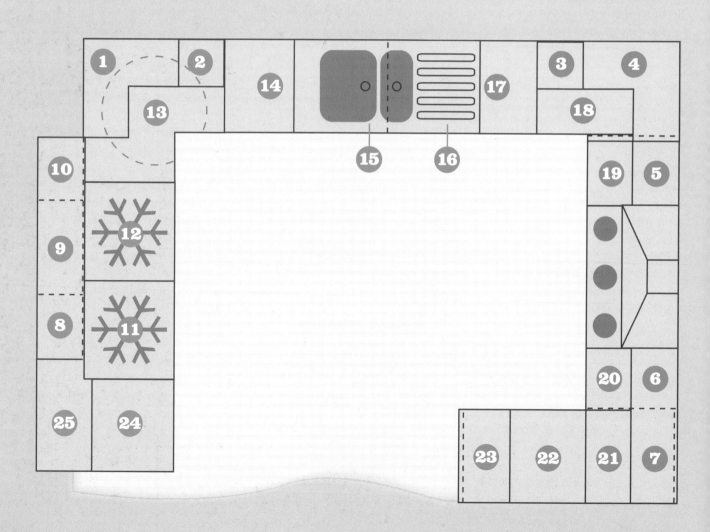

(Left, above and below) The finished kitchen is a stylish, spacious and practical space. The combination of traditional and modern materials – oak, granite and stainless steel – ensures that the new extension blends in with the rest of Rose Cottage.

Rose Cottage Kitchen Shopping List

UNITS

1 Wall corner 625 x 625
2 Wall 300
3 Wall 300 (for everyday china)
4 Wall corner 625 x 625 (for everyday china)
5 Wall 400 (for everyday china)
6 Wall 400 (for condiments, sauces)
7 Wall 600 (for glass)
8 Wall 400 under counter (for best china)
9 Wall 600 under counter (for best china)
10 Wall 400 under counter (for best china)
11 Integrated freezer
12 Integrated fridge
13 Carousel unit (food storage)
14 400 drawer-line base
15 Base 600 sink (for cleaning materials)
16 Integrated dishwasher 600
17 400 drawer-line base
18 Carousel unit (food storage)
19 Base 400 with drop-forward bin
20 Base 400 (for pans)
21 Base 600 (access from passage)
22 Base 500
23 Base 300
24 Storage for microwave oven and integrated wine rack
25 Wine rack

ADDITIONS

Granite worktop
Cornice 3 x 3m lengths
Pelmet 2 x 3m lengths
Plinth 4 x 3m lengths
End panels x 4
Handles x 26
Carousel x 1

APPLIANCES

Integrated dishwasher
$1\frac{1}{2}$ bowl undermounted stainless steel sink
Integrated fridge-freezer
900 range cooker
900 chimney hood

✳ Kitchen Fitting Work Schedule

✔ **PRELIMINARY**
Identify kitchen electric circuits
Ensure cold stopcock works
Ensure hot gate valve works

✔ **CHECK OUT PROFESSIONAL HELP**
Suitability
Availability
Terms

✔ **ASSESS TOOL REQUIREMENTS**
Purchase
Hire

✔ **MAKE BUILDING CONTROL APPLICATION FOR PART P** (see pages 155–156)

✔ **ALTERATIONS INVOLVED**
Draw plans
Make planning permission application (to be combined with building control application)
Finalize agreement with builder and adjust time schedule accordingly

✔ **COMMITMENT**
Confirm purchase of kitchen units
Confirm purchase of new appliances
Shop for lighting
Buy new tools
Buy plumbing parts
Buy electrical parts
Buy sundries

✔ **ARRANGE HIRE**
Tools
Skip

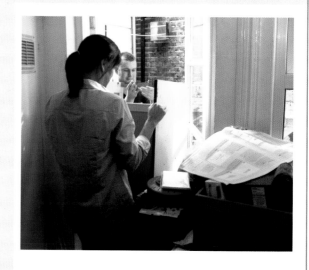

✔ **SCHEDULE TRADESMEN**
Plasterer
Plumber/Corgi registered gas fitter
Electrician
Tiler

✔ **WORK BEGINS**
Clear space to store deliveries *(below left)*
Check deliveries carefully
Re-order any missing parts
Re-assess time schedule

✔ **POINT OF NO RETURN**
Clear kitchen cupboards and store contents
Organize temporary facilities for cooking, refrigeration and washing up

✔ **RIP-OUT SEQUENCE**
Remove and dispose of old kitchen units *(above)*
Make good/room preparation

✔ **INSTALLATION SEQUENCE**

✔ **FINISHING OFF**

Kitchen Planner

Use the grid below as a starting point for planning your kitchen. Make some enlarged photocopies of this page (enlargements of 150% fit onto A3 paper) and use one copy to draw up the final plan of your kitchen on, making sure it is to scale (one square = 20mm). Then cut out the example cabinets and appliances you want to include from some of the other copies. You can move these around on your room plan to try out different layouts.

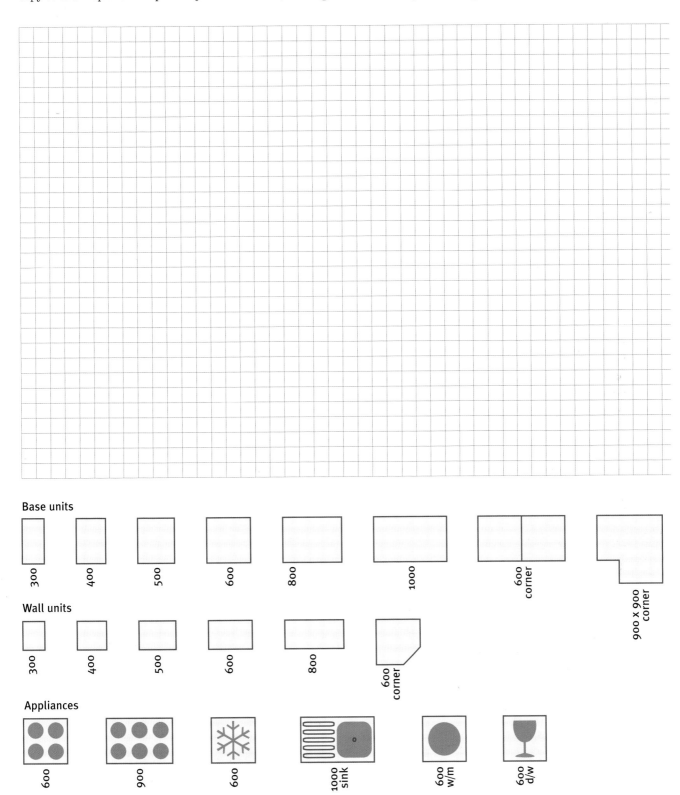

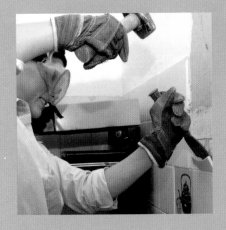  

2 Removing the Old Kitchen

Now that you have planned your future kitchen to perfection, it is time to get rid of the old to make way for the new. Careful removal and thorough preparation are important: they will make installation of the new kitchen a much easier and smoother process.

Preliminary Work

As soon as the purchase decision is made there are jobs that can be done to save time later. Kitchen electrical circuits as well as the controls for the hot and cold water should be checked. When work starts it will be extremely annoying to be held up because a valve will not work.

An application to the local authority Building Control department may have to be made, professional tradesmen must be booked and arrangements should be made for the disposal of the debris.

Finally, do you have the right tools for the job? If there are stubborn tiles to remove or pipes going through the cabinets, a trip to the tool hire shop may be called for.

WATER PUMP PLIERS

When faced with undoing a particularly stubborn valve then use a pair of water pump pliers but use with extreme care. The valves are made of brass and this is a soft metal that does not take kindly to force. Grip the shaft tightly, not the handle, close to the body of the valve and apply a tiny vibration action, just enough to loosen the scale.

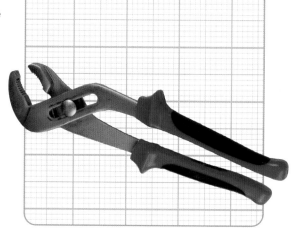

do it CHECK WATER VALVES

Ensure the water can be turned off before work starts. Turn off the cold water at the main stopcock **A**, which is usually under the kitchen sink. The hot water valve **B**, should be in the airing cupboard. Look for this gate valve on a 22mm pipe coming from the cold water cistern in the loft to the bottom of the hot water cylinder. The pipe will feel cold. When the water supply is turned off the reduction in pressure will stop the flow of hot water coming out the top of the cylinder. Sometimes this takes a few minutes. It is good practice to give these valves a turn once a year. Make a note in your diary for the autumn.

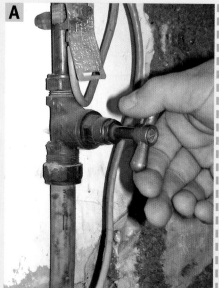

IDENTIFY CIRCUITS AND FUSES

A little investigation work on the electrical system will also save time. Even if a previous electrician has labelled the fuses in the consumer unit they should be checked to ensure that the identification still applies. See also page 158.

HOW TO IDENTIFY CIRCUITS

There are three circuits that are usually present in a kitchen:

CIRCUIT	COLOUR	REWIRABLE FUSE[†]	MINIATURE CIRCUIT BREAKER
Ceiling light *(sometimes includes cabinet lights)*	White	5amp	6amp
Ring main *(sockets and appliances)*	Red	30amp	32amp
Cooker *(dedicated radial circuit)*	Red	30amp	32amp

[†] found in older-type consumer units

1 Identify each circuit by pulling out the fuse or switching off the MCB **A**. First of all, eliminate the cooker supply by switching on the oven light and then turning off each 32A MCB in turn until it goes out: cookers below 3kW – a single oven, for example – should be fitted with a 13amp plug and plugged into the ring main. Replace the fuse on each unsuccessful attempt.

2 Plug in and switch on a radio and remove the other 32A MCBs until the radio falls silent **B**. Having identified the circuit, plug the radio into all the other sockets to confirm they are all on the same circuit. Similarly, switch on all the lights, including any cabinet lights, and turn off each 6A MCB until you find the one that turns off the ceiling light. If the cabinet lights stay lit they will be connected to the ring main circuit.

3 Do not make any assumptions unless you have an intimate knowledge of your house's history. When identifying fuses check all the sockets in the kitchen to be sure that they are all on the same circuit. For example, if a house has been extended a new ring main could have been installed to avoid connecting to the original ring. Subsequently, the division between the new extension and the house may have been removed to form an open-plan kitchen/diner. The result is that the kitchen area has two ring mains.

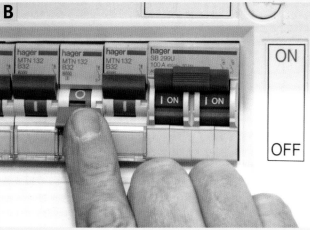

Disposing of the Old Kitchen

Every year, many tons of waste goes into landfill as the result of refurbishments around the home. You have a responsibility, both legal and moral, to make sure that your old kitchen is disposed of safely and the elements from it reused or recycled where feasible. Ask yourself, before you fill a skip with chipboard and laminate units that will end up as part of our environment, whether you really need to throw it all away, or whether it could be put to use in some other way. For example, it may not be necessary to replace the wall or base unit carcasses just because you don't like the style of the doors. Most kitchen units are made to similar dimensions and you could save yourself time, effort and money, and be easier on your conscience, if you just replace the fronts.

A decision must be made in advance about what to do with the elements of the old kitchen that you do decide to throw away. Inevitably, there will be units beyond redemption. In any case, there will be packaging material from the new kitchen as well as debris. There are three choices. You may decide to deal with this by making regular trips to a local authority recycling yard; you could make arrangements with a private contractor who specializes in waste disposal; or you could hire a skip.

Ways to Reuse the Old Units

4

SELL THEM ON If you are only replacing your old units because they are not to your taste but they are essentially in good condition, you could try selling them through your local paper. This will also solve the problem of how to dispose of them as the buyer will probably come to collect them. Bear in mind, though, that some damage while removing the units is inevitable: pull them out first and see what you are left with before placing your advertisement.

BE A GOOD NEIGHBOUR If you live on an new-build estate it is worth canvassing neighbours because the chances are that all the kitchens on the estate came from the same supplier. Someone may be very grateful for a couple of extra units that are a perfect match for their kitchen.

USE THEM FOR STORAGE Recycling a few units to the garage or shed is worth consideration. Wall units in particular, provide excellent storage for some of the paraphernalia that seems to accumulate around the home. Even if you don't have a garage or shed yourself someone else might want to buy them for theirs.

USE THEM DURING THE REFURBISHMENT As they are likely to be of an identical height, old wall or base units make excellent improvised workbenches while you're putting together the new kitchen. Use two or more as sawhorses when you cut longer pieces such as the worktop or plinth.

Cover up
Ripping out an old kitchen can be a dirty job and it is wise to take precautions before work starts. Protect floor coverings with dustsheets along the traffic routes. Set aside an area outside for the temporary storage of the rubbish. Anticipate approximately 6 cubic metres from an average kitchen.

CAUTION SKIP HIRE

■ As long as the carcasses are broken down, a 6-yard skip should be adequate for an average kitchen.

■ If a skip is to be parked on the road then you must apply for a skip licence from your local authority.

■ The skip must be marked by amber flashing lights either placed against the skip or attached to each corner of it.

■ There must be traffic cones on the approach side of the skip to guide the traffic safely past. It is usually the responsibility of the hire company to provide the lights and cones.

doit THE RIP-OUT

In the majority of cases the sequence that follows will get the job done in a logical, efficient manner.

Doors, Shelves and Drawers

1 Start by taking off all the doors 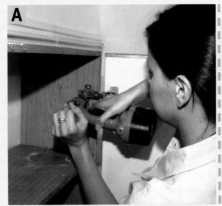 and removing the internal shelves which will probably not be fixed. Then remove the drawers 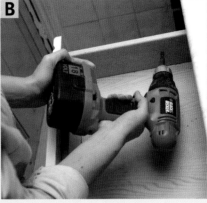.

2 After the cabinets are stripped it is easier to see any services installed inside. Plug sockets supplying appliances can be identified and dealt with and pipework under the kitchen sink will be accessible.

toptip*

Keep back a couple of drawers. They are useful for containing and carting out the debris especially when the wall tiles are removed.

Electrical Connections

In the interest of safety it is sensible to get all of the electrical work out of the way before the floor gets wet. Therefore deal with the electrics before the plumbing.

1 Isolate the supply by turning off the main switch. Remove the fuse to the circuit you will be working on. Confirm that the circuit is dead by using a circuit tester  before touching the cable connections (see page 158).

2 Disconnect any sockets installed in the cabinets and unthread the cables from the units .

3 As a temporary safety measure, wire any tail ends into a connection block and tape it up to protect tiny inquisitive fingers . Or you could fit a junction box.

Gas Connections

The only job involving gas that can be done by an unqualified person is the removal of the hose used to connect a freestanding cooker to the gas supply. All other work must be done by a Corgi registered gas fitter.

The hose is attached to the gas pipe at the wall by means of a bayonet connection. It is disconnected in a similar way to removing a bayonet light bulb: push in and turn to the left. The bayonet valve is spring-assisted and designed to close immediately the hose is removed. The valve to turn off the gas will be found adjacent to the gas meter.

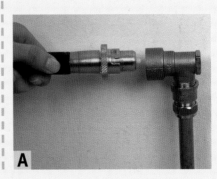

Washing Machines and Dishwashers

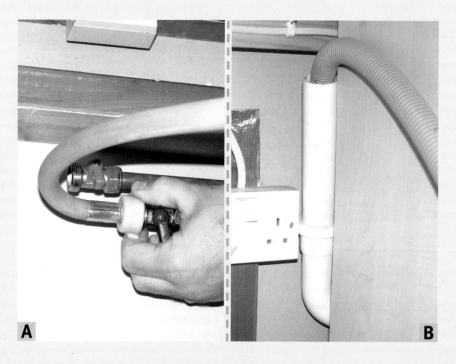

A

B

1 These appliances have flexible hoses, colour coded red (hot) and blue (cold), attached to valves on the water supply pipes by means of screw-on caps. To shut the valve, turn the on/off lever 90° so that it is set at a right angle. It is then just a matter of unscrewing the hose **A**.

2 There is usually a grey flexible hose, approximately 20mm diameter, for the waste discharge. This may be pushed into a standpipe: a vertical 40mm pipe that connects to the waste system via a trap **B**. Or, the hose may be attached to a spigot on the sink P-trap. To remove the hose it is only necessary to loosen the Jubilee clip that holds it in place.

Hoods and Extractors

Whatever the version, the electrical connection should follow the same principle. Just like other appliances they must be connected to the ring main via an FCU (fused connection unit) or a conventional three-pin plug (see also page 164).

toptip*

A little detective work may be required to undo the extractor. For example, with chimney hoods you may have to remove the chimney cover to reveal some of the hidden fixings. With integrated extractors it may be necessary to first remove the swivel-slider panels attached to the door in order to find the fixing screws. Look for the spring clips that release the panels.

Cabinet Lights

1 Remove the fuse that isolates the cabinet lights. Do not rely on the switch alone.

2 When absolutely certain that the circuit is dead, cut through the cable next to the light, remove the light fitting **A** and unthread it through the old cabinets. Redundant cables should be traced back and removed or, as a temporary measure, a connection block should be fitted to the free end, then protected with electrical tape **B**.

A

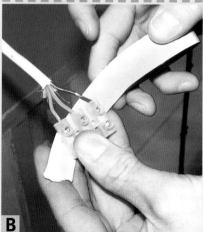

B

Wall Units

1 Begin by checking that all the internal shelves have been removed **A**. They will add to the weight of the carcass and could be dangerous if they fall out when the carcass is moved.

2 Remove the cornice and pelmet if there is one. These two items are not just decorative – they also hold the carcasses together. The cornice is usually screwed directly into the carcass from above. The pelmet is attached from behind using assembly blocks or small brackets.

3 Each carcass will be connected to its neighbour either by interconnectors or simply by wood screws, sometimes hidden behind the hinge carriers **B**. The cabinet interconnectors are male/female bolts that pass through each side of the adjacent carcass gables to screw together and pull them up tight.

4 Older cabinets may be fixed to the wall using long screws, one through the back of the carcass in each corner **C**. More recent cabinets employ an adjustable hook and wall-bracket system. Look for plastic boxes with two adjustable screw heads, in each of the top corners of the cabinet. One of the adjustment screws is used to loosen the carcass from the wall bracket.

5 All that is then required is to lift the carcass off its brackets **D**.

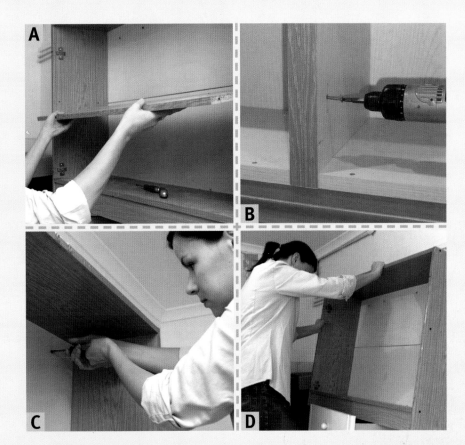

CAUTION REMOVING WALL CARCASSES

■ There are potential dangers in taking down wall carcasses. The sudden shift in weight can take you by surprise and this could be quite hazardous especially if it happens when up a ladder.

■ As a precaution, lay a small carcass or stack of drawers that you have removed upon the worktop. This will take the weight when you remove a wall carcass (see right). A 500mm-wide carcass is especially useful because this is the usual distance between the worktop and the underside of the wall units.

■ If the carcass is strong enough, keep it aside for later use when the process has to be reversed. It could also come in handy as a seat, sawhorse and hop-up while the refurbishment takes place.

The Sink

1 When the taps are disconnected the area will get wet and when the waste trap is removed the smell could be nauseous. Therefore, to avoid unpleasantness, undo the clips that hold the sink to the worktop before touching the plumbing because this job will entail lying on your back under the sink **A**.

2 After the hot and cold water has been turned off (see page 56) open the taps. Be prepared for it to take a while before the water stops running. The hot water can take ten minutes before it is reduced to a slow dribble. An old towel can be quite useful for mopping up and keep a couple of push-fit stop-ends at hand to cap the pipes and staunch the flow of water. If you use a pipe-slice to cut the pipes **B**, then the job can be done quickly.

3 Finally, the only thing holding the sink is the waste pipe and this is undone by turning the topmost plastic collar anti-clockwise **C**. It should turn using hand pressure alone. Place a bucket underneath the pipe to catch the dirty water.

4 If the sink has been sealed to the worktop using silicone it will be necessary to run a knife round the top flange. The sink should now release from the worktop **D**.

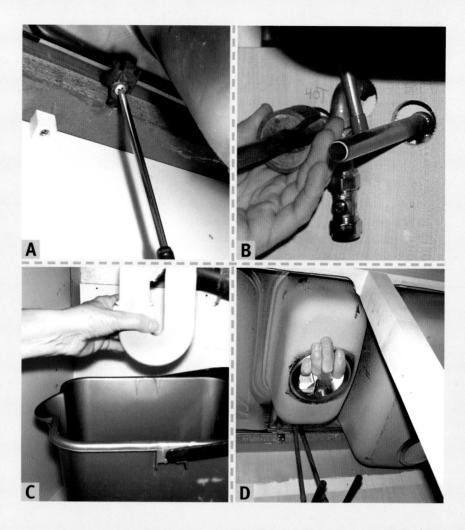

A   B

C   D

PIPE-SLICE

The easiest way to cut copper pipe is with a pipe-slice. This produces a clean, square cut with a rounded edge (see also page 148).

toptips*

Before the cold water is turned off, fill the kettle or a couple of empty plastic bottles so that you still have drinking water while you work.

When hot and cold water pipes are disconnected it is a good idea to identify them using red or blue electrical tape. Although it may be obvious which is which at the time, this may not be the case in a day or so.

Wall Tiles

It is much easier to remove wall tiles when the area is completely clear of cabinets. However, you may find that they have to be taken off at this stage in order to release the old worktops.

The degree of difficulty that this job entails depends on the adhesive that was used and, perhaps more significantly, it depends on the wall itself. The most difficult of all are tiles that were put on using a strong sand/cement mortar. Fortunately this practice had largely died out by the 70s and may not be encountered very often. Look for large, 6-inch square white tiles. Also, it is most likely that the wall will be built of solid masonry.

1 Before removing the tiles, switch off the power and loosen the screws on any electrical fittings within the tiled area, such as plug sockets and fused connection units. The tiles will extend to a short distance behind the accessory plate and any leverage could break the fitting. You will need a club hammer and bolster as well as the usual safety gear of goggles for eye protection and gloves to protect the hands from the sharp edges of the broken tiles **A**.

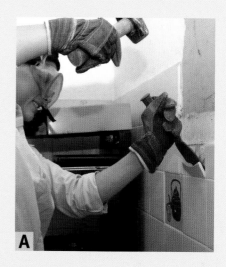

A

toptip*

If it is not necessary to remove the tiles in order to free the worktop, you may not have to take them off at all. New tiles can be laid on top of old tiles.

Dealing with Damaged Walls

Walls made of plasterboard can be a problem because the surface of the board may tear off when the tiles are removed. It may help to reach behind the tiles and cut away the adhesive using a stripping knife but be prepared for a damaged patch or two. If the surface card facing peels away it is not much of a problem but if you end up with a large hole in the board it will take a little longer to put right. Minor damage can be repaired quite easily using surface fillers. There are several patching plasters that can be used but best of all is a product known as Bonding. All these products are prepared by mixing with water until a thick paste is achieved. It can then be spread over the damaged area to the same thickness as the board surface.

When tile removal results in a large hole and the wall is a stud partition it will be necessary to apply a patch on the other side of the plasterboard. The ideal material is another piece of plasterboard but other types of firm boards can be used. First, tidy up the hole by cutting away any ragged bits and enlarging the opening into an ellipse or oblong shape **A**. Next, cut the patch material so that it is larger than the hole and of a similar shape. Cut a hole in the centre of the patch large enough to get your finger through **B**. Apply a suitable 'no nails-type' adhesive to the facing edge of the patch. Pass the narrow end of the patch through the wide part of the hole, turn it round and pull it forward using your finger through the centre so that it covers the hole and the adhesive engages with the hidden side. Hold it there until the adhesion starts to work. When it has properly cured (allow 24 hours) the section can be filled with patching plaster **C** then smoothed down when the plaster is dry.

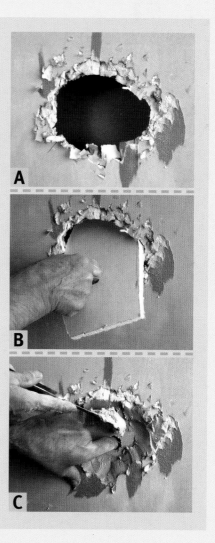

A

B

C

Worktops

1 If the worktop has been sealed to the wall with a silicone fillet, cut along it with a sharp knife. Then remove the screws that secure the worktop onto the base units **A**.

2 Use an old handsaw to cut through any narrow sections of cutouts left from the hob and the sink to break it up into manageable pieces.

3 Finally, deal with the joints between the different sections. The work surface should now lift off easily and can be removed **B**.

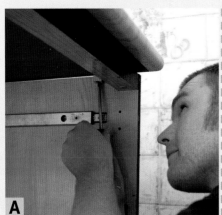

Problems with Worktops

The most difficult problem is pipes that have been installed through the worktop after the kitchen was installed. The usual culprit is a wall-hung boiler and this means that besides the water pipes there may also be a gas pipe to deal with. Proceed with extreme caution and do not do anything that will jeopardize the integrity of the gas pipe.

The best way to sort this out is to cut away the section of worktop holding the pipes. First check the area immediately below to verify that none of the pipes branch to one side. Drill a hole (of at least 12mm) about 100mm away from the pipes as a starter hole for an electric jigsaw **A**. Cut around the pipes leaving a safe margin **B**.

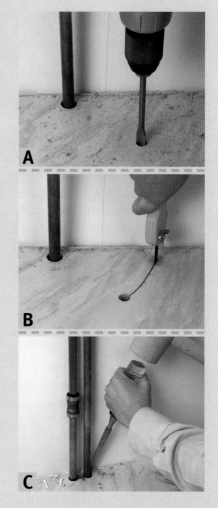

If you do not have a jigsaw, an alternative is to drill a series of holes as close to each other as possible and then to cut away the material between using a padsaw. This will allow the bulk of the worktop to be removed without interfering with the pipes. When all the old kitchen units have been taken out you will be in a much better position to deal with the remaining piece of worktop.

If a gas pipe is involved it may be possible to leave the whole thing until the gas fitter is called in later on in the project (when a gas appliance is installed). If there are only water pipes and they are not part of the central heating, then the problem should be tackled whilst the water is turned off. It may well be expedient to simply cut the pipes to free the remaining piece. Otherwise, very carefully cut it away with a wood chisel. Try to keep the sharp end of the chisel facing away from the pipes (and yourself) **C**.

Base Units

1 The first job is to remove the plinth or kick-board. The plinth will either be screwed to the carcass gables or secured by some type of spring clip.

2 The base carcasses will be connected to each other and to the wall. Once the worktop has been taken off the connections should be easy to locate. As with the wall units, screws used to join adjacent units may be hidden behind the hinge plates. In other cases the screw heads may be concealed by a plastic insert. The connection to the wall is usually by means of an angle bracket **A**. Sometimes the back panel of the carcass can be slid out in order to make the wall brackets accessible. Once all the fixings are removed you can pull the base unit away **B**.

toptip*

If kitchen units are to be disposed of, an easy way to break them up is to drop the carcass from shoulder height onto one of its corners. The carcass will usually break apart into its component bits. Obviously, sensible precautions must be taken while doing this.

The Sink Unit

The most difficult cabinet to deal with is usually the sink unit. Of necessity the final pipe work would have been installed after the unit was fitted and therefore will prevent the cabinet lifting out. Sometimes the cabinet can be freed just by cutting back the pipes but in most cases you will need to dismantle the carcass where it stands and deal with each panel a piece at a time **A**.

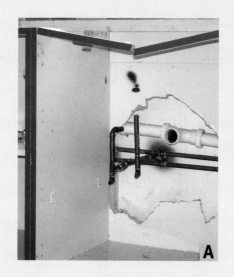

toptip*

Stuff a piece of rag down the waste pipe. This will help stop drain smells percolating into the house and protect the pipe from falling debris.

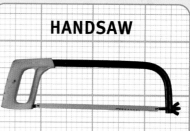

HANDSAW

Should it be necessary to shorten the remaining waste pipe use an old handsaw. Handsaws are ideal for cutting through plastic waste pipes because they leave a nice straight cut that can easily be tidied up with a file.

Floor Coverings

Floor coverings are normally installed after the kitchen units and therefore may only extend to the underside of the plinth. If you intend to keep the existing covering check that the plinth on the new base units is not set further back than the old one. This will result in an unsightly gap.

toptip*

A plinth can be set further forward by mounting the attachment clips on pieces of batten fixed to the back of the plinth. However, this will make the plinth more prominent and reduce the kickspace for feet.

1 Vinyl floor coverings are glued to the floor substrate. Vinyl tiles can be prised up using a stripping knife. If the adhesive has set hard it may be necessary to tap the end with a hammer **A**. Alternatively, try using a heat gun to soften the glue **B**. Direct the nozzle back and forth 150mm away from the surface and while it is still warm use the stripping knife to lift the material from the floor.

2 Floor tiles are notoriously difficult to take up. They are usually stuck down with a cement-based adhesive and this can be hard work to loosen. In this case, hire a suitable SDS electric drill.

doit TIDY UP

With the old kitchen cleared away you will be able to stand back and take stock. Remove any old wallpaper and flooring that you do not want to keep and dispose of it *(below)*.

Any loose ends that were temporarily ignored now require attention. Besides having a jolly good clean-up you will need to make the electrics and plumbing safe so that fuses can be reinserted and the water can be turned back on.

Electrical Connections

Double check the work you did to remove the electrical appliances. If cables were cut as a matter of expediency now is the time to disconnect the trailing ends from the cable outlet plates. Where a cable simply comes straight out of the wall temporarily make the end safe by fitting a connector block and wrapping it in electrical tape, or use a junction box **A**.

toptip*

With the room clear of obstructions you have the opportunity to carry out work that may be more difficult when the new kitchen is installed. If the walls are in poor condition, such as loose plaster or badly torn plasterboard, call in a plasterer. If you are intending to install recessed downlighters in the ceiling, the job may entail fixing an additional skin of plasterboard below the existing ceiling. It will be much easier to carry this out when the room is empty.

Plumbing

The pipework may have been severely cut back in order to remove the old cabinets. As a consequence it may be necessary to make some temporary arrangements so that the water can be turned back on while you decide on your next course of action. Providing the pipe was cut using a pipe-slice, push-fit fittings can be used with confidence. See page 147.

1 On the hot water pipe fit an isolating valve **A**. This will allow the hot water to be turned on again without flooding the kitchen and avoid having to turn it off again when the pipework is extended to the new sink.

2 As for the cold water, there should be sufficient water stored in the cistern in the loft to maintain the supply to the house for some time. If, however, the plumbing is not likely to be completed for a day or two, it is advisable to make a temporary connection between the stopcock and the rising main. Fit a coupling on the rising main and another on the incoming supply and join the two with pipe **B**. Then turn on the stopcock to fill the cistern.

A

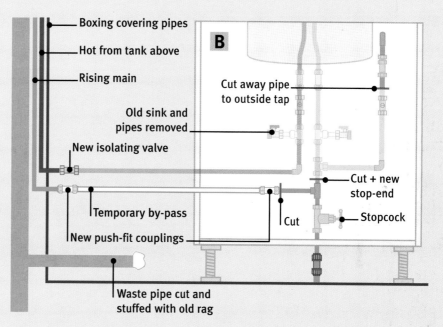

Boxing covering pipes

Hot from tank above

Rising main

B

Cut away pipe to outside tap

Old sink and pipes removed

New isolating valve

Cut + new stop-end

Temporary by-pass

Cut

Stopcock

New push-fit couplings

Waste pipe cut and stuffed with old rag

STEEL WOOL

When making connections to old copper pipe use steel wool to clean away old paint and grime.

Inspect the Existing Pipework

When additions and alterations have been made over several years the resultant pipework may have come to resemble Spaghetti Junction. You will need to consider if any section is worth saving. The main issues will be the condition of the pipe and fittings and whether the existing configuration will impede any part of the new kitchen layout. Check the pipe to make sure there are no kinks or dents. Inspect the joints looking for tell-tale green marks. These indicate old leaks and although they may no longer be active they add an element of risk.

3 Installing your New Kitchen

The installation is a three-part exercise.

First check the area to make sure the kitchen

will fit as planned. Next, do the room preparation

to get all the dirty jobs out of the way.

Finally, build and fit the kitchen units.

A Kitchen Survey

Once the room is clear, a thorough survey should be carried out. With all the obstructions out of the way the dimensions can be verified: the walls can be checked for plumb; corners measured for square; and the floor assessed for level. Walls that looked perfectly true, corners that appeared to be at right angles and a floor that seemed to be even, may be found to be quite the contrary when subjected to a proper check.

toptips*

If you do not have a large builder's set square to check the room for square corners open up one of the flatpacks and improvise with the corners of a large shelf or a gable.

If you do not have a long spirit level for measuring the floor you can improvise with a long piece of timber that will not flex and is perfectly straight (a 50 x 25mm batten should do the trick). Use masking tape to attach your spirit level in the middle of the narrow side. Check the accuracy of the instrument by reversing it and reading it again.

CAUTION
COOKER SWITCHES

It was not until the late 1980s that the electrical regulations required cables to be installed in 'safe' zones (see page 165). If your house was built prior to 1980 check for cables buried in diagonal runs; especially from the cooker control switch to the cable outlet. The arrangement shown below, for example, would seriously contravene electrical regulations.

doit MARK UP LIVE CABLES

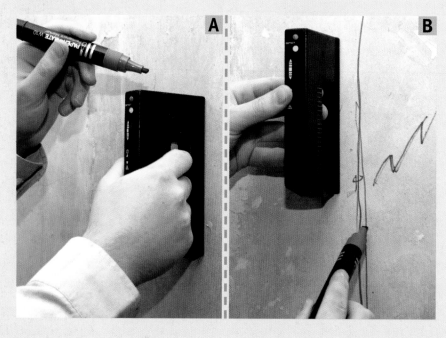

Now is the ideal time to sweep the kitchen walls with a metal detector to check for hidden dangers **A**. Mark any 'live' contacts to alert you to the potential hazard **B**.

doit SETTING OUT

1 If any run of base or wall units is going to be a tight fit check the distance between the walls at three different heights. The measurement at worktop height **A** should verify the dimension used on the plan. Measure again about 2m above the floor **B** to make sure the wall units will fit. Finally, compare the measurement just above the floor **C** to ensure the base units will fit.

If either measurement **B** or **C** is significantly different from the plan dimension measurement **A** this may indicate that the walls are out of plumb and could pinch the layout. A solution must be found and the plan reworked before going any further.

2 Next, use a spirit level, at least 1200mm long, to check how level the floor is. Lay the spirit level about 500mm away from the walls – this is the path that the plinth will follow and therefore the reference line for the height of the units **D**. Do not measure at the base of the wall where the floor may be a different height than at the front of the units and therefore give an inaccurate starting point.

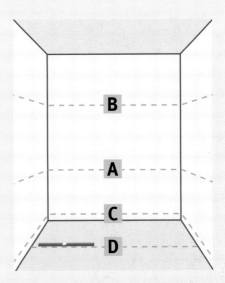

Assessing the Floor Level

Assess the difference in height between the highest and lowest points of the floor. Suppose this difference is 20mm. If the datum line (see page 72) is based on the cabinets standing at the lowest spot on the floor the plinth will have to be tapered by up to 20mm in order to fit beneath them. Conversely, if the cabinets are set at the highest point in the floor there will be a gap of up to 20mm between the top of the plinth and the underside of the carcasses **A**. Note that the plinth should be flush to the floor, rather than the underside of the cabinets. If the floor is to be tiled some of the gap above the plinth could be lost by thickening the adhesive where the floor falls away.

The plinth is set back from the front of the carcass by about 50mm. Another 20mm can be added for the thickness of the door, making the total overhang about 70mm. This should mean that a small gap between the plinth and cabinets is not seen. However, if the gap occurs at an exposed end it will be more apparent. In these positions the plinth return does not have an overhang and a 20mm gap would be quite noticeable. Therefore if any exposed ends coincide with a low part of the floor, the floor level at this position should be used to establish the datum point. Another solution would be to add an end support panel and abut the plinth to it **B**.

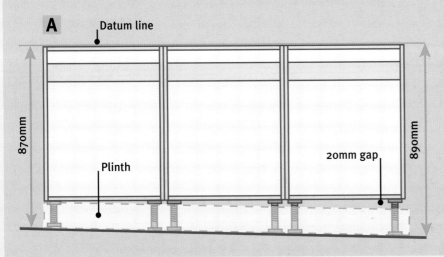

A — Datum line — 870mm — Plinth — 890mm — 20mm gap

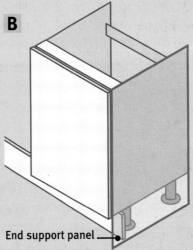

B — End support panel

doit MARK THE DATUM LINE

1 The datum point will be the height to the top of the base carcass plus the thickness of any floor covering to be put down later on. For example, a base carcass may be 870mm high. If ceramic floor tiles are to be laid, allow a further 12mm for the tile plus the adhesive. The datum level is therefore 882mm above the floor at the chosen position. Mark it on a piece of batten or the edge of a spare panel **A**.

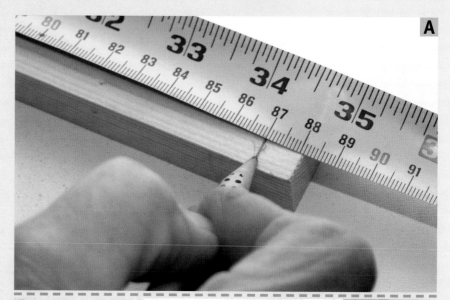

2 Hold the batten upright and transfer the height to the wall using a spirit level **B**. Accuracy is important because it will be used to set the heights of all the kitchen units.

3 Using a long spirit level draw a horizontal line round the walls, level with this datum mark **C**.

4 To make the fitting stage easier, mark the wall with the position of each unit and each fixed appliance. The centre line for a focal point, such as a hob with an extractor above, will take precedence. Find this position and then work outwards keeping the first wall units equidistant from the line. Using full-scale dimensions, mark a short vertical line on the wall to represent the edge of each unit. Remember to include support panels and try to keep fillers of equal width to achieve a balanced look.

toptip*

When marking a line around a room using a spirit level, swap over ends after marking each line to compensate for any inaccuracy in the level.

First Fix Electrics

The preparation for the electrical installation must be done before the new kitchen can be fitted. The electrician will need to check out the existing installation to make sure the circuits and equipment are not faulty and are capable of handling the increased load. Any safety faults that are discovered must be corrected before the new work can proceed. Redundant accessories and cables will be removed and the existing installation adapted to suit the new kitchen plan.

Preparing the Route

Most electricians will be prepared to accept someone else doing some of the preparation work. If the new cable runs are chased in and the walls prepared with the new metal boxes it will cut down the time spent by the professional electrician and will therefore save you money. According to Building Regulations, vertical chases must not be deeper than one third of the wall thickness (34mm); horizontal chases no deeper than one sixth of the wall thickness (17mm).

FIT WALL SOCKETS

1 To keep the kitchen uniform, the new sockets should be set at the same height as existing electrical accessories but when there is no precedent, a centre line set at 1200mm above floor level is a good guide. Mark a horizontal centre line and use this to position the galvanized metal box that will be let into the wall **A**.

2 Sweep the area with a metal detector to make sure there are no pipes or cables hidden below the surface. Turn the box over and hold it so that the line dissects the screw holes for the front plate. Then draw round the box **B**.

3 Use an electric hammer-drill fitted with a masonry bit to drill a series of holes round the pencil line to the depth of the metal box. Cut out the waste material using a club hammer and bolster chisel. Try not to over-enlarge the cut out **C**.

4 Place the box in the cut out and mark two fixing positions at the back of the box. Use a 6mm masonry drill and two red wall plugs to make the fixings **D**.

Continued on page 74

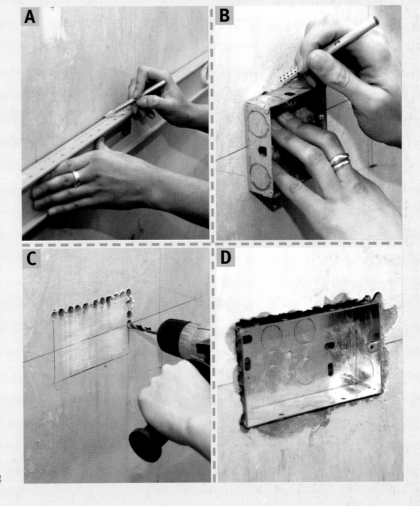

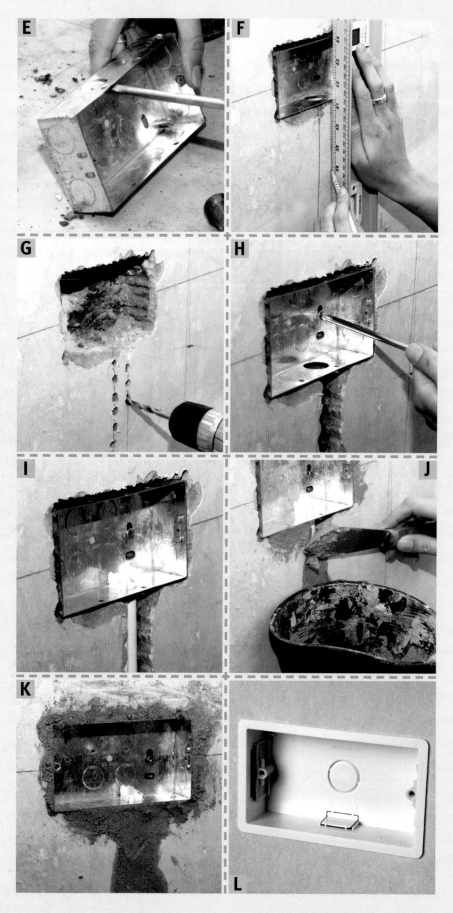

5 Knock out one of the bottom holes suitable to accept the cables and mark this position on the wall below the cut out **E**.

6 Draw two parallel lines down the wall from the hole to approximately 100mm below the datum line marked on the wall. The lines represent the sides of the chase **F**.

7 Use the electric drill to perforate the sides of the chase ready for cutting out the waste material with the bolster **G**.

8 Fit the galvanized box using two 4x25mm screws **H**.

9 The 2.5mm twin and earth (or T&E) cable can be put in at this stage if they are ready to be linked round between the various points. Protect the cable from the rough edge of the hole using a rubber grommet. Use cable clips to hold the cables in the wall chase until the filler has set.

10 If the cables are to be installed later on, make provision by fitting plastic conduit. Cut two lengths of small oval conduit intended for single cables. Fit them side by side with the top ends pushed into the hole in the galvanized box and the other ends wedged in place using masonry nails **I**.

11 Use a suitable filler to make good and set the box and conduit/cables in place **J**. It is important that the galvanized box is totally secure. The filler should be used to stop lateral movement that would weaken the screw fixings **K**.

12 Where a socket is to be installed in a hollow wall, cut away an aperture in the plasterboard and fit a dry-lining box **L**.

do it CABINET LIGHTING AND EXTRACTORS

1 A simple method of providing a power supply for cabinet lights or an extractor is via a plug and socket, located inside a base unit so that it is hidden but accessible. Mark its location using a spirit level (see pages 72–73). Chain drill the sides of the channel, ready to cut out **A**.

2 At the 'first fix' stage all that is necessary is to bury a small plastic conduit in the wall running vertically from the extractor position (or from the bottom of the wall cabinet position) to below the datum line, ready to take a round flexible cable. Leave sufficient cable at the top to reach the fitting and at the bottom to reach the plug socket **B**.

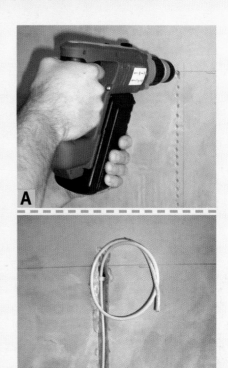

top tip*

The three-pin plug should be fitted with a 3amp fuse.

Accessories Fitted in Cabinets

A job that is perfectly suited to someone who is not a qualified electrician involves preparing the kitchen units for the electrics. It is preferable to leave this until the cabinets have been installed but before the worktops are fitted. Plug sockets and other accessories fit onto surface-mounted plastic boxes called 'pattresses'. Normally they are fitted high up on the back rail of a base unit and in this position the cables enter through the back knock-out.

However, if the accessory will not be accessible on the back, the pattress box can be adapted for the cables to enter at one end and be fitted on one of the gables towards the cabinet front. For a neat finish, a short length of box conduit can be attached to conceal the cable between the back of the unit and the pattress box. When they have all been fitted, make sure there is a clear pathway for the electrician to thread through the cables and make the connections.

CABINET FIXINGS
Drill the hole for the wires through the back panel. Fix the pattress box near the top of one gable and attach the box conduit, ready for the electrician to thread through the cables.

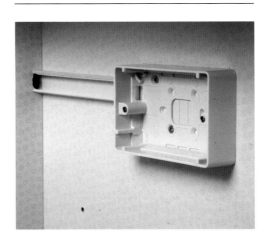

top tip*

Electrical regulations now require every new installation to be fitted with an RCD (residual current device). If your house has one of these be prepared for the whole system to trip out when cables are cut. Separate the wires and reset the RCD at the consumer unit.

First Fix Plumbing

Cold Water Supply

From a practical point of view it is logical to group all the plumbing connections under the kitchen sink, where there has to be a hot and cold water supply for the kitchen tap. This pipework can be utilized to feed wet appliances as well as any outside tap.

The Stopcock

If the stopcock is in the kitchen make sure it will not interfere with any of the appliances and that it will be accessible after the new units are installed (see *Positioning Plumbing Services*, page 45).

Integrated dishwashers require a lot of room. There is only about 20mm of free space between the back of the machine and the wall, except at ground level where a space is created when the machine is raised

toptip*

By international convention the cold water tap is always on the right and hot on the left. Be aware of this when organizing the pipework.

on its legs. Take accurate measurements and with luck it may be possible to install the machine over an offending stopcock and add a secondary stopcock downstream in an accessible position. However, there may be no other alternative than to move it. This is not beyond the reach of a competent DIY enthusiast but does involve specialist tools and parts. It would be better for the gas fitter to deal with it, if and when a gas hob is installed.

Provision for the Sink

At some stage after the stopcock there must be a branch off (or tee) to the kitchen tap (see box below). This tee should be installed now and the pipe extended to the position where it will enter the sink carcass. Fit a temporary stop-end so that

Anatomy of **Under-Sink Plumbing**

Typically, the cold water supply enters a house under the kitchen sink. A tee provides a supply to the kitchen tap before the rising main takes the fresh water to a tank in the loft. All three types of fittings: push-fit, compression and solder are shown for illustrative purposes only.

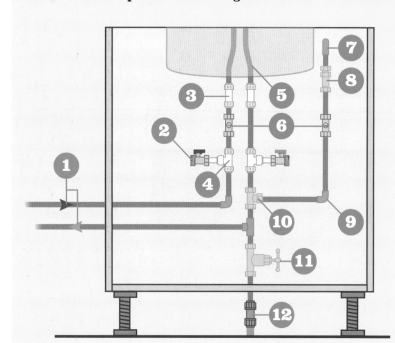

1 Water flow direction (hot and cold)
2 Washing maching valve
3 Push-fit (Speedfit) straight coupling
4 Push-fit (Speedfit) tee fitting
5 Soft copper tails from monobloc sink tap bent into Y shape
6 Isolating valves
7 Pipe through wall to outside tap
8 Check valve
9 Copper 'end-feed' elbow
10 Compression tee fitting
11 Stopcock
12 Incoming cold water supply (blue 25mm medium density polyethylene pipe + adaptor to reduce to 15mm copper pipe)

the water can be turned on for the rest of the house without flooding the kitchen. Eventually this branch can be made to supply cold water to any wet appliances as well as to the sink. These connections will be made inside the sink unit at second fix stage. All that is required for now is to decide if the cabinet will be dropped down over the pipe or enter through the back panel. If the stopcock is not located under the sink a service valve will be needed so that maintenance can be carried out without affecting the rest of the house. Fit the service valve in place of the stop-end.

Hot Water Supply

The hot water pipework is more straightforward. From where the pipe enters the kitchen from the hot water cylinder, it will eventually need to be extended to the tap position. If this cannot be done immediately, block off the hot water by fitting an isolating valve on the incoming pipe. This will enable the hot water to be turned back on for the rest of the house and avoid the system being closed down when the time comes to work on the pipe.

The only appliance that may require hot water is a washing machine and the connection for this can be added at second fix stage. The latest washing machines are like dishwashers, in that they only require a cold water supply.

Drainage Preparation

Foul water from the kitchen sink and wet appliances must be discharged into the foul drain that leads to the sewer. It must not go into the drain used by rainwater pipes. Sometimes there is a drainage gully installed outside for this purpose but it is more commonly connected to a soil stack pipe (SSP). This is a 100mm diameter pipe used to carry the effluent from bathroom to the foul drain. If the bathroom is situated above the kitchen the pipe will probably be hidden inside vertical boxing in one corner (see also pages 144–145).

 Rules for Drainage

✔ Discharge into a drainage gully is very straightforward. All that is required is a neat hole at an appropriate place through the outside wall big enough for a 40mm pipe *(above right)*. The pipework can be left until second fix stage.

✔ When connection to the SSP is necessary, it may be possible to utilize the old pipeway. Usually a 40mm plastic pipe will have been used and this will enter the SSP by way of a rubber seal. The old waste should be pulled out and replaced with the new pipe. See also *Kitchen Plumbing*, pages 144–154.

✔ When the distance to the kitchen sink is more than 3m the waste pipe will need to be increased to 50mm diameter to comply with the regulations. If the old connection to the SSP only allows for a 40mm pipe it will have to be blanked off and a new entry formed. Look for a 'boss' low down on the pipe. This is a protrusion ready-made for the purpose but it needs to be cut through into the SSP and a 'boss socket adaptor' has to be glued to it using solvent-weld cement (see page 153). Before the waste pipe is joined to the sink it must be reduced back to 40mm.

✔ The waste pipe should have a fall of 18–90mm per metre run and should be clipped to the wall at least every metre.

✔ Where and how the waste pipe enters the sink cabinet must be considered because once the units are fitted the pipe will not be accessible. Ideally, the waste pipe should enter the cabinet parallel to the water pipes so that the cabinet can be lifted over the pipes if they enter from below *(above left)*, or slid over the pipes if they enter through holes in the back.

✔ Most base units have a service void that will accommodate a 40mm waste pipe clipped to the wall. As long as it is fitted tight to the wall and the connections are formed using solvent-weld fittings, the pipe will not impede the base units. Cut out a section of the gable to fit the cabinet over the pipe.

Washing Machine and Dishwasher Wastes

The most convenient place to fit a wet appliance is adjacent to the kitchen sink. Not only will this make it easy to connect to the existing water supply but it will also enable the waste hose to be connected to the sink waste. If the machine is to be installed further away – too far for the hose to reach the sink trap – the waste can be dealt with by using a standpipe or a saddle clamp (see below).

③ Ways to Connect Appliances to the Waste

SPIGOT Providing they are situated close to the kitchen sink, the easiest way of connecting a dishwasher or washing machine discharge hose to the drainage system is by attaching them to the sink waste trap. There are special P-traps that incorporate washing machine spigots (see also page 152). The flexible hose from the machine is pushed over the spigot and held in place using a jubilee clip. The hose must enter the spigot from above to prevent waste water from the sink stagnating in the pipe **A**.

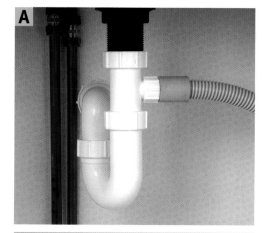

STANDPIPE A standpipe can be purchased in ready-made kit form or made up from a 600mm long section of 40mm solvent weld waste pipe fitted into a P-trap capable of hosing a telescopic inlet. These traps are often referred to as washing machine traps. If possible fit the standpipe adjacent to the machine because if it has to be fitted behind it will, of course, push the machine forward so that it will no longer fit under a standard 600mm worktop. Where this is unavoidable, use a 650mm worktop and fit the run of base units 50mm out from the wall **B**.

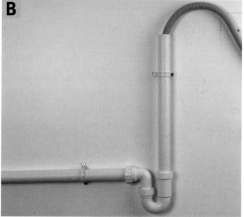

SADDLE CLAMP If neither system can be used, there is a special kit called a saddle clamp that can be attached to the waste pipe at any convenient position. The main feature is a saddle that clamps round the pipe. The flexible hose from the machine is attached to a spigot and this is connected to the saddle using an elbow. A tool is provided with the kit to cut a hole into the waste pipe. A check valve is incorporated to prevent siphonage back to the machine. Although the fitted kit still sticks out from the wall it is less obtrusive than a standpipe and it may be possible to fit it behind a cabinet where it will not obstruct the machine **C**.

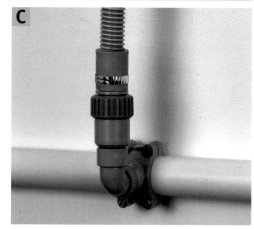

Extractor Preparation

If the plan includes an extractor vented to the outside, it is sensible to cut the hole through the exterior wall at this stage. Not only will the work be easier when nothing is in the way but it will also avoid debris scratching the cabinets. The downside to this is that some very careful measurements must be taken to ensure that the hole ends up in the right place. If the extractor is located on an outside wall the hole can be made immediately above the fan mechanism. The centre line of the extractor/hob can be used to centre the hole. The height will depend on the type and size of the extractor and its height above the worktop.

Anatomy of an Extractor Location

The height of integrated extractors is predetermined because they are designed to fit between two wall units. With chimney hoods there are no such restraints.

If the extractor is to be fitted above a gas hob the minimum distance between the worktop and the under side of the extractor is 650mm. However, both the hob and/or the extractor manufacturers may specify a wider gap than this so it is essential to check their recommendation before making a decision. In any case, for many people 650mm may seem too low because the extractor ends up at face level, but the wider the gap the less efficient the extractor will be.

If, say, a height of 700mm is decided, measure this distance plus the thickness of the worktop (say, 38mm) above the base unit datum line = total 738mm. Draw a horizontal line at this point. This will be used later as the base reference for the chimney hood template. It should be at least 1610mm above the floor. Unpack the extractor and measure the height to the top of the fan mechanism. Mark this distance on the wall above the base line. If there is any doubt, temporarily fit the extractor on the wall (see pages 80–81).

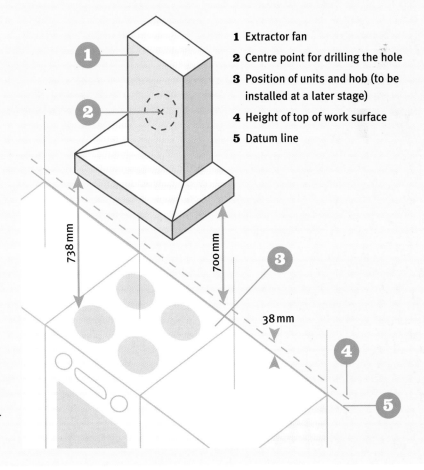

738 mm

700 mm

38 mm

1 Extractor fan
2 Centre point for drilling the hole
3 Position of units and hob (to be installed at a later stage)
4 Height of top of work surface
5 Datum line

do it CUT THE HOLE FOR AN EXTRACTOR

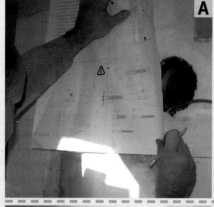

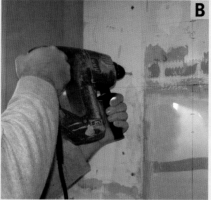

1 Check the outside face of the wall for obstructions before making the hole (see below). If you need to fit the extractor temporarily, draw the base line using a spirit level. Align the template supplied with the base and centre lines **A**.

2 Mark the fixing holes through the template onto the wall. Drill the holes according to the manufacturer's specification **B**. Fit the extractor and check it is level. Mark the position of the hole using the duct as a template **C**. If the extractor will get in the way, draw round it and take it down again.

3 Drill a pilot hole from the inside through to the outside. Use a masonry bit at least 260mm long and 8–10mm diameter in an electric hammer drill. Ideally, there should be a slight fall towards the outside so that any dampness will run away **D**.

Dealing with an Obstruction

When there is a potential obstruction it will be necessary to pinpoint the hole on the outside of the wall. The easiest way to do this is to relate the position of the hole to a nearby window or door and then to measure backwards on the outside of the wall.

Start by measuring the height of the hole from the inside **A**. Using a spirit level (or a laser) transfer the height to the door or window **B** and mark it on the outside brickwork. Measure the distance to the opening and deduct a 12mm allowance for the thickness of the plaster. Using the brick course as a guide, measure this distance back from the corner brick. Mark the wall with a piece of chalk. If the hole coincides with an obstruction, the clearance distance can be measured and a corresponding adjustment made on the inside.

In the case of a chimney hood, the hole can be moved within the confines of the chimney providing it does not interfere with the fixings. In the case of an integrated extractor, it can be moved sideways within the 600mm width and/or raised as long as it is hidden by a cornice.

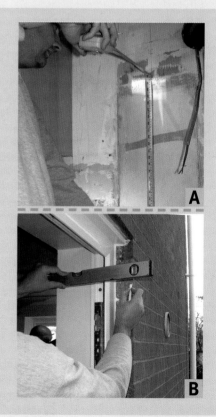

4 The cheapest and most common form of extractor kit uses a flexible plastic tube for the duct. The duct should go from the exhaust hole of the extractor, through the wall and into a louvre vent on the outside.

With the pilot hole as a reference, use one of the parts supplied (such as the duct spigot) as a template for marking up the hole **E**. The position of the hole may have to be adjusted so that the edges do not come close to the edges of the brick. If the brick margin is too thin it could break away, making the hole too big.

5 For the best result, use a masonry core cutter of a slightly larger diameter than the duct **F** and **G**. They must be used in an SDS drill with an automatic clutch that disengages the drive shaft if the cutter gets stuck. The drill and cutter are usually hired together.

The alternative is to use a hammer drill and masonry bit. Chain drill holes around the circumference of the duct hole **H**. Cut out the centre with a club hammer and bolster chisel.

NOTE Take care not to allow debris to fall into the wall cavity where it could bridge the gap and enable damp to penetrate to the inside. If the cavity contains insulation material cut this away with a knife.

6 Repeat the same process on the inside to complete the hole.

7 Temporarily place the outer vent plate in the hole, align it with the brick courses, and mark the four fixing holes on the wall. Using the 6mm masonry bit, drill holes to the same depth as the wall plugs.

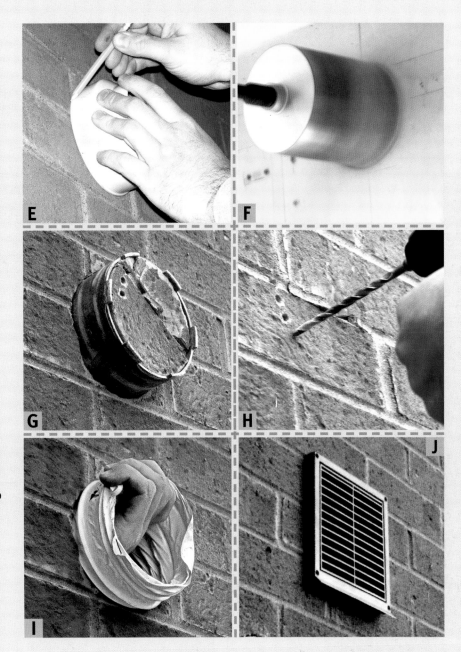

8 Feed the flexible duct through the hole, taking care not to tear the plastic, until there is about 100mm surplus on the outside **I**. Attach the vent plate to the duct and fix it in position using non-rusting screws **J**. The remainder of the duct can be left on the inside until the extractor is installed.

toptip*

When a hole is drilled through a sheet material the other surface is likely to splinter or fray when the drill bit erupts. Brickwork behaves the same way. The brick on the far side will fracture as the drill breaks through. To minimize the effect use a sharp drill bit and decrease the pressure as it reaches the surface.

CUT A DUCT THROUGH AN ADJACENT WALL

If the extractor is fitted on an internal wall, a ventilation duct can be run along the top of the wall units to an adjacent outside wall. Be aware that if the distance is more than 3m the extractor will lose efficiency.

The flexible plastic tubing used for direct ducting should only be used for the initial connection because it can be crushed or torn when left exposed. Rigid kits are available instead, which comprise of oblong box-section tubes that slot together. The shape is similar to a house brick so that if a brick is removed from the outside wall the tube can be fitted through the gap.

1 At an opening in the outside wall (such as a door or window) mark the level of the base unit datum line with a pencil or piece of chalk **A**.

Inside the kitchen, measure the distance between the datum line and where the top of the wall units will be **B**, using standard dimensions (see page 80). Transfer this measurement to the outside brickwork and mark it with a piece of chalk **C**, measuring up from the datum line mark. Unless this mark happens to coincide with the bottom of a brick, mark the next brick course above it to avoid having to cut small pieces of brick.

2 Now, from the inside measure the distance from the door or window edge to the corner of the wall **D**. Transfer this measurement to the outside, working from the door or window edge, along the brick course marked with chalk. From this point, the next whole or half brick back towards the opening should be the position of the hole through the wall **E**.

3 Use a voltage detector to sweep the walls inside the kitchen, at the corner where you are going to drill.

4 From the outside, drill a pilot hole through the mortar at the bottom corner of the brick using a long, thin drill bit. It should be at least 260mm long and 8–10mm diameter.

5 Check the pilot hole on the inside; when the brick is cut out and the hole extended through the wall the pilot hole should be in a suitable position for the duct. Cut out the brick using the same technique as on page 81. Then, using the long drill bit, make a couple of holes through the inside blockwork to mark the corners of the hole on the inside face. Complete the hole from the inside and tidy up. The preparation is now complete.

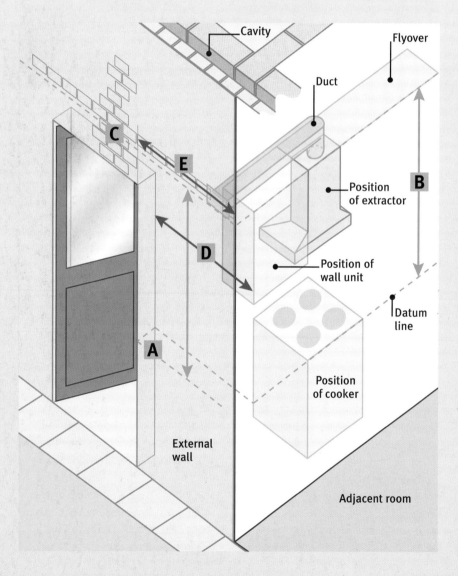

Cavity

Flyover

Duct

Position of extractor

Position of wall unit

B

C

E

D

A

Datum line

Position of cooker

External wall

Adjacent room

Flat-Pack Cabinets

Although cabinets are unique to each manufacturer there are, nevertheless, several common features. They are designed to be as versatile as possible with fixings hidden from view. Standard doors are often interchangeable between base and wall units. The end panels or gables can usually be switched between one side of the carcass and the other. Common fixings and fittings are used throughout the range.

Floorstanding cabinets have a base panel to which adjustable legs are attached. Gables are pre-drilled to take the fixings, hinges and shelf supports. They attach to each side of the base panel to form the basis of the carcass and this is held together at the top with a couple of rails. Stability comes from the back panel (sometimes two). This slides down a groove cut into each gable and locates into a similar groove cut into the base panel.

Wall carcasses have interchangeable top and bottom panels as well as end gables. They join together in the same way as base units to form four sides of a box. Once again, the back panel fits into a groove running round the back inside edge of the panels and this stabilizes the unit.

top tip*

The packaging from flatpack cabinets can be useful so do not discard it immediately. The cardboard can be used to protect the floor of a walkway in place of a dustsheet. Look out for suitable material for protecting the worktops later on.

Anatomy of a Flat-pack Base Cabinet

Self-assembly kitchen units come with a set of instructions that are specific to the carcass and will show the steps required for the construction. These should be referred to for the detail. Whilst it would be impractical to attempt to cover the same ground here, a general overview of the flat-pack base cabinet may be helpful.

1 Front and back rails

2 Gable

3 Back panel

4 Gable

5 Instructions

6 Hinges, dowels, brackets

7 Adjustable legs

8 Base panel

9 Shelf

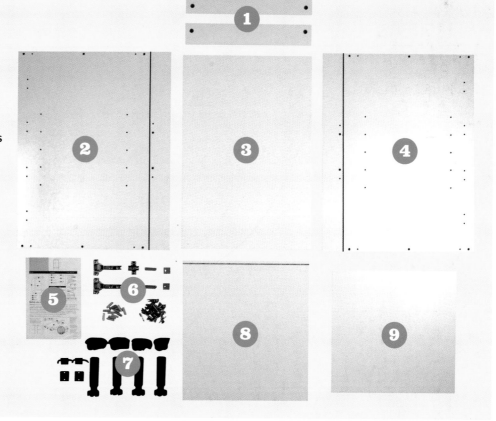

do it · ASSEMBLE FLAT-PACK CARCASSES

1 Open the flat-pack. Identify all the components, check them off against the contents list and make sure none are damaged **A**. Normally there is a plastic bag containing small parts such as cams and shelf supports. Empty these into a bowl where they will be readily accessible. Store the door hinges out of the way until they are needed near the end of the project.

2 Start the assembly process with the gables. Lay them out back to back so that one becomes the right gable and the other the left. Gables are usually designed to be reversible so that they can be used at either end.

It is surprisingly easy to make up the first gable as the right-hand side and then to make up the other, also as a right-hand side **B**.

It is far easier to insert all the fiddly small parts when the gable is lying face down and at waist height rather than after the unit is installed when poor access and light will hamper progress. As the first gable is prepared consider all the fittings that could be added. For example, a base gable can have worktop fixing blocks, screw-in dowel pins, wooden dowels, wall fixing brackets, shelf supports, and plastic hole-plugs. Leave door hinges and buffer plates until after the carcasses are installed.

3 Next, insert all the cams into the base panel and rails on the 'blind' side. Make sure they are left in the 'open' position to accept the metal dowel pins. The orientation is indicated by an arrow **C**.

4 To build the unit lay one gable flat and add the base panel, front and back rails. It helps to clamp the gable to the workbench. Lower the panels onto the gable so that the metal dowel pins engage with the cams **D**. Insert a No. 2 Posidrive screwdriver into the face of each cam and turn it approximately 150 degrees clockwise to fully tighten on the dowel pin head and pull the two panels together.

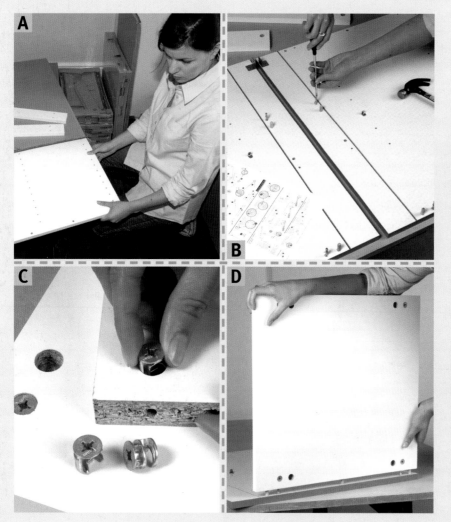

toptips*

Although it is possible to assemble units on the kitchen floor, it is much easier and kinder on the knees and back to do it on some form of workbench. A Black and Decker Workmate is useful for smaller units or the units themselves can be used providing care is taken. A kitchen table would be ideal, especially for tall units.

Have a couple of bowls to one side; one for sorting through the bag of small parts, the other for collecting the surplus small parts.

Where units are installed with an exposed gable the outside colour should be changed to match the general trim colour of the kitchen. Some manufacturers provide add-on gables in the trim colour. Others provide replacement gables. If your cabinets use substitute gables consider the final location of each unit and replace the gable as soon as the carcass is unpacked.

When the carcass is complete the cams should be on the blind side **E**.

All 1000mm base units have a centre post that should be fitted in conjunction with the front rail. Make sure the post is not back to front. Also, some 1000mm corner base units are designed to accept different size doors. Those intended for a 400mm or a 600mm door will need to have the muntin post fitted accordingly.

5 Locate the remaining gable onto the assembly and lock the cams onto the dowel pins **F**.

6 Slide the back panel into the housing groove at this stage **G**.

7 Complete the assembly of the base units by fitting the legs **H**. See *Adjustable Cabinet Legs*, above.

8 Finally, stand the unit on its feet and slide in the shelf. Resist the temptation to fit the door.

ADJUSTABLE CABINET LEGS

The legs for base cabinets normally come in two pieces: a housing and the adjustable leg itself. Most types of housing have a centre post that pushes into a pre-drilled hole in the underside of the base panel.

Be aware that if the housing is not symmetrical it may have a protrusion that is intended to lend support to the gable. If your cabinet legs are designed like this, make sure that the front legs have the protrusion pointing towards the back of the cabinet. It may interfere with the plinth if fitted facing the wrong way.

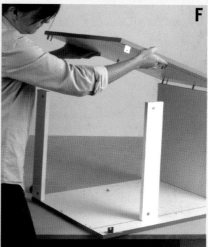

toptip*

It will be quicker in the long run to construct all the carcasses in one session. The base units will usually be installed first, starting from one corner. If storage is limited, leave the wall units and make up the base units in reverse order so that the last one to be put together is the first corner unit to be fitted.

doit INSTALL BASE UNITS

1 Just before fitting the first cabinet have a closer look at the wall where the units are to be installed. A house where the walls are straight and perfectly upright is rare indeed; the older the house the greater the irregularity. In order to achieve a professional finish it may be necessary to adjust the carcasses to compensate for discrepancies. See pages 88–89 for how to do this.

2 Start fitting the cabinets working out from a corner. Place the first corner cabinet in the corner and adjust the height by turning the legs until the top of the carcass is in line with the datum line (turn clockwise to raise) **A**. Checking the level with a long spirit level make the final adjustments. Use the spirit level to check the cabinet alignment, not only

side to side and back to front but also on each diagonal **B**. An undistorted cabinet should form a box with each corner a perfect right angle. Therefore, when the cabinet top is perfectly level the sides and front will be perfectly vertical. Take a little extra time on the first cabinet because this one can be used as a reference for the others.

NOTE If a 1000mm base cabinet is used in a corner, to be fitted (later) with a 500mm door, leave a 100mm gap between the end gable and the return wall. A special corner post must be fitted in the middle of the unit so that it can link with the return run of cabinets and the open side blanked off.

If the corner base unit is to be fitted with a 600mm door, the corner post should be fixed 400mm from the end and the gap to the wall widened to 200mm.

3 The cabinet must be firmly screwed to the wall through a fixing bracket at each side (see *Stretcher Plates*, left). Stand the cabinet in position. If it has been properly prepared it will stand without rocking, with the top perfectly level and the top back corners of the gables touching the wall at the datum line. Make a pencil mark through a slot in each bracket onto the wall **C**.

4 Remove the cabinet and sweep the wall with a metal detector to ensure there are no hidden cables or pipes **D**. Using a 6mm masonry bit drill a hole through each mark to take a suitable fixing, deep enough for the screw **E**. See *Fixings*, page 94.

STRETCHER PLATES

The preferred bracket for fixing units to the wall is sometimes confusingly called a stretcher plate. This has two holes on one flange for attaching it to the carcass and two slots on the other flange for fixing it to the wall. Make sure that the corner of the plate is in line with the back face of the gable.

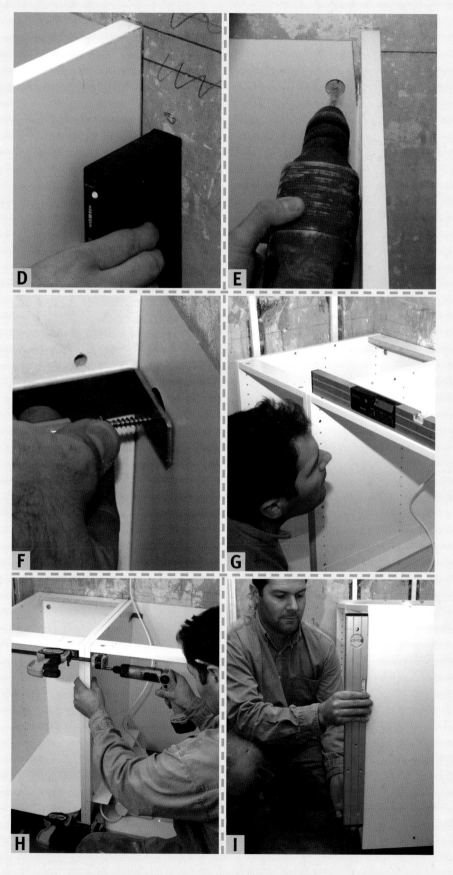

5 Realign the cabinet and fix using 4mm or 5mm (No.8) screws at least 30mm long. Double check that the cabinet is properly positioned **F**.

6 Work away from the corner adding cabinets and levelling them as before, this time using the first cabinet as a reference. Level each new cabinet to the one before and keep an eye on the datum line to verify that no discrepancy has crept in **G**.

7 After each cabinet is fixed to the wall it must be fixed to the previous one. Drill a 4mm clearance hole through the centre of each hinge position or door buffer position towards the previous cabinet. Using a clamp, hold the gables of both cabinets perfectly together and join them using 30mm long 4mm screws through the holes **H**. If the carcass is only 15mm thick take care not to over-tighten the screws.

8 Check the front faces for accuracy with a spirit level **I**.

toptips*

Cut a piece of batten 600mm long to act as a spacer guide for integrated appliances. This is more accurate than using a tape measure alone.

When joining two cupboards together with screws, one of the boards must be pre-drilled with a clearance hole. This allows the screw to turn freely and draw the other board in to make a tight fit.

INSTALL CABINETS ON IRREGULAR WALLS

An inexperienced kitchen fitter may not be aware of the effects caused by bulging walls. By using a few packing pieces in the right places the cabinets can be made to fit in perfect alignment. It is not until the worktops are installed that the implications become obvious and by this time it is too late to do anything about it.

To produce a smart professional finish it is important not only to get the cabinets level but also to make sure that the gaps and overhangs are even. If suitable adjustments are not made at the start for imperfections in the walls, the worktops could end up out of line and this may detract from the effect that you want to achieve.

Ideally, the back of the worktop should follow the line of the cabinets in order to create an even 25mm overhang at the front but if a bulge in the wall at one end has pushed some cabinets forward, creating a gap, it may be difficult to follow the line. In any case, the worktop may have to be fitted close to the wall to remain square with an adjoining worktop and this could make it impossible to maintain a consistent overhang. Usually the worktop will taper along the run of units. Pay particular attention to this when long runs of units are present.

The problem is simple to overcome providing it is tackled when the cabinets are installed. Each cabinet will be fixed to the wall with a bracket just below worktop level. This is the only part that needs to touch the wall. The gable below can be cut away without affecting the stability of the cabinet and with the excess removed the unit will not be pushed forward by the wall.

Some professional kitchen fitters prepare each carcass in this way, regardless of the wall conditions.

The bottom part of each gable can be removed quite quickly using a jigsaw. Not only does this avoid discrepancies in the wall but it also enables the cabinet to pass over any cables and pipes behind.

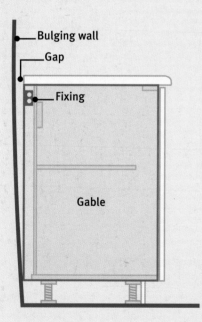

Bulging wall
Gap
Fixing
Gable

Bulge in wall forces cabinet forward

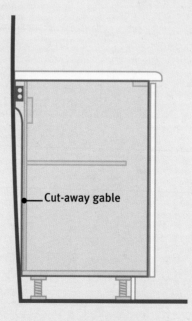

Cut-away gable

Cut away gable allows fixings to touch wall

ADJUST CABINETS FOR A BOWED WALL

Walls sometimes have a small bow midway along the wall that make them appear to be slightly concave or convex **A**. Test this by holding a long straightedge against the wall at worktop height. If standard cabinets are fitted against a bowed wall the run of units will follow the shape. On a convex wall this will cause the cabinets to splay out **B**. Not only will there be implications for the worktop but there will also be gaps between the cabinets at the front.

To preserve the alignment some adjustment to the top of the carcass will be necessary.

For example, if the wall is concave the middle cabinets can be fitted as normal but the gables of the cabinets to each side should be cut back in graduations to suit the bow in the wall. On concave walls the middle cabinets must be cut back **C**.

Packing Out

An alternative solution would be to use packing behind some of the fixing brackets. However, this will ultimately create a gap between the back of the worktop and the wall. In moderation the use of packers is acceptable practice. For example, when the wall is to be tiled the thickness of the tile plus the adhesive will bridge the gap. However, if the packing distance reaches 5mm alarm bells should start to ring and an alternative method should be used.

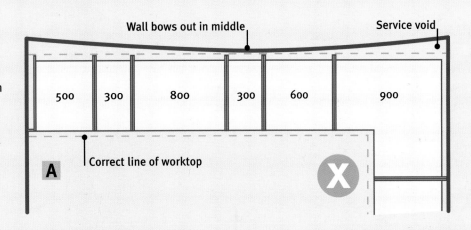

Wall bows out in middle | Service void

500 | 300 | 800 | 300 | 600 | 900

Correct line of worktop

A

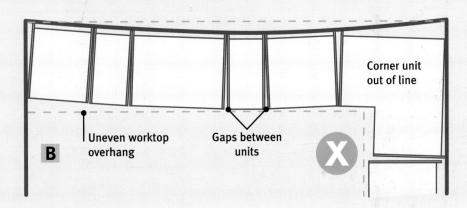

Corner unit out of line

Uneven worktop overhang | Gaps between units

B

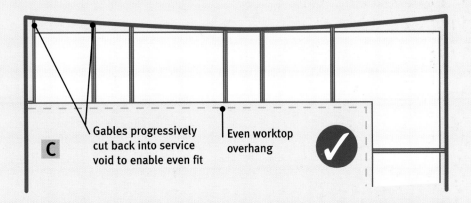

Gables progressively cut back into service void to enable even fit | Even worktop overhang

C

Installing Tall Units

Tall units are cumbersome and help will be needed in order to move them. Owing to their weight it is easier to lower the unit into alignment than to raise it. Therefore extend the legs prior to standing it up and lower it into position by winding the legs anti-clockwise.

Tall Units for Housing Built-in Appliances

If an oven is to be fitted into a tall unit do not rely on the standard shelf assembly to hold the weight of the appliance. Fix support battens on the cabinet gables below the shelf (see below).

If an integrated fridge/freezer is to be installed it is essential to increase the air flow at the back of the unit to enable the appliance to work efficiently. Leave out the cabinet back panel and then cut away the rear of the top panel to create a gap of at least 50mm to the wall. A ventilation space of similar dimensions must also be left in the plinth.

BUILDING UP
Attach the four horizontal panels to one gable. Slide the back panels to the top and bottom compartments, then add the other gable.

OVEN SUPPORT
Reinforce the shelf support by adding a batten below on each side.

toptip*

If they are extended fully cabinet legs will become unstable and could break. For height adjustments higher or lower than 10mm, stand the legs on off-cuts of material or cut them down.

CAUTION TALL UNIT SAFETY

■ Do not attempt to manoeuvre a tall cabinet into an upright position using its legs as a pivot. The weight of the unit is likely to break the fixings.
■ Tall units are inherently unsteady and rely on the adjacent cabinets and/or the wall fixings for stability. They should be fixed to the wall approximately 1.5m above the floor.

Installing Peninsular and Island Units

These are formed from a line of base units, fixed together without the benefit of a wall to stabilize them. A large matching panel has to be fixed to the back of the units to cover the exposed carcasses. Normally this is taken down and scribed to the floor and if a raw edge is showing it will have to be finished with iron-on tape. Back panels should be fitted with concealed fixings. Spring clips, flush mounts or panel-fixing mounts are all suitable for this purpose. In each case it is essential to make careful measurements.

BREAKFAST BAR
With the addition of stools, this peninsular unit can be used as a breakfast bar.

do it MARK UP FOR WALL UNITS

The default height for wall units is governed by tall or dresser units. If either of these cabinets is included in the plan, the top of the wall units must be set in line with the top of the tallest unit **A**. Mark a line on the wall at this height. You can then use this line as the basis for marking up where the cabinet fixing plates should be placed **B** (see *Fit the Wall Units*, page 92). The bottom of the wall units will then be approximately 500mm above the worktop.

If the kitchen only includes dresser units (see page 29) the fixing lines for the wall units must be accurately set out using the manufacturer's recommended distances. The dresser units cannot be installed until after the worktop has been fitted because they sit on the worktop.

If neither type of unit features in the plan then the wall units can be set to any convenient height.

do it   FIT THE WALL UNITS

1 Wall units are made up in a similar fashion to the base units except that the back panel is slid into a groove before the other gable is fitted **A**. A wall hanging bracket is attached to the top corners of the unit **B**.

2 Strike a new datum line to represent the top of the cabinets. Mark another line below this to represent the level of the fixing holes for the wall plates. The distance depends on the type of wall hanging system used in the cabinet range **C**.

3 Starting in a corner, mark off the width of each cabinet working along the two horizontal lines. Mark the positions of the fixing plate holes following the manufacturer's recommended distance. Set this out from each side of the lines that indicate the edges of the cabinets **D**.

4 Sweep the wall for hidden dangers before drilling (see page 70). Then plug and fix the wall plates **E**.

5 As for base units, wall units are fitted working outwards from a corner. Using a No. 2 Posidrive screwdriver extend the adjustable bracket in the top corner of each unit so that the hook part protrudes

CABINET HANGERS

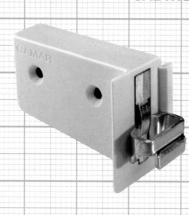

There are two types of cabinet hanger available. The type shown on the left is fitted inside the cabinet, fixed to the top corners of each gable so that the hook protrudes through the back panel. A recent innovation is shown in B above. This sort is fitted into holes at the back of each gable and locked in place by pulling down a lever. Both versions hook onto a wall hanging plate and have two screws to adjust them in and out, and up and down.

beyond the back of the unit **F**. This will increase the chance of attaching the unit to both brackets first time.

6 With the vertical lines as a guide, lift the unit above the top line and slide it down the wall until the brackets locate onto both wall plates. Make sure the hook has engaged behind the wall plate and is not merely resting on top of it **G**.

7 The orientation of the cabinet is adjusted using the screws in the bracket. Use the height adjustment screw to bring the top in line with the datum line. Check it with a spirit level and then tighten the other screw to draw the cabinet into the wall and lock it there. If the wall is not straight it may be necessary to use some form of packing behind the cabinet **H**.

8 Adjacent wall units are connected in the same way as base units. Clamp the cabinets together so that the gables line up. Drill a 4mm hole through the hinge positions of one cabinet, making sure the other gable is not penetrated. Use 30mm long, 4mm screws or an interconnecting bolt (see box, below). Use a spirit level to check the front face for vertical alignment. A small lean can be corrected using a little packing.

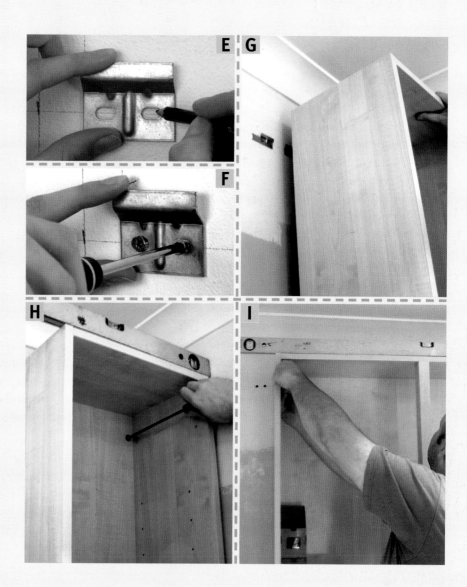

toptip*

Lifting wall cabinets into position can be quite strenuous, particularly if the fixing hooks do not engage first time. Lighten the task by removing the shelves. If there is no one to assist, lay a 500mm wide cabinet across a board on the base unit below to act as a staging post.

INTERCONNECTING BOLT

The contents of flat-pack units often include special bolts for connecting two cabinets. The female side of the bolt is pushed into a hole (5mm for metal type shown, 10mm for plastic), drilled through two adjoining gables and the male end is screwed in from the other side. Alternatively, the cabinets can be joined using 4mm chipboard screws inserted through clearance holes. Hidden fixings can be created by drilling the holes behind the hinge position.

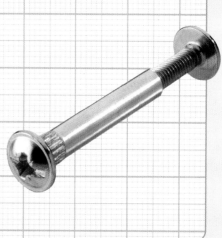

Wall Fixings

Fixing cabinets and appliances to walls is a fundamental aspect of kitchen fitting. It can usually be accomplished using a basic electric drill equipped with a hammer setting and a couple of different sized masonry drill bits. The technique is simple but it is important to choose the correct fixings as any attempt to economize or make do could lead to expensive, heart-breaking consequences.

The type of fixing will depend on the job it is doing and the construction of wall to which it is fitted. In the case of a floor standing unit the downward force is taken care of by the floor and most of the lateral stability is achieved by attachment to other units and the weight of the contents. The fixings only need to be light/medium duty. Wall-hung units are just the opposite. They rely on the fixings because they do not get any support from the floor and the weight of the contents adds to the liability. Medium/heavy duty fixings have to be used.

Wall Assessment

Building techniques and materials are forever changing and the construction of the walls will to some extent depend on the age of the house. Older houses are more likely to have solid walls made of brick or partitions made of lath and plaster. After World War II, breeze blocks, made from furnace clinker, began to replace bricks inside houses. Later these were superseded by aerated concrete blocks; a grey, homogeneous soft material. More recently, in order to reduce the drying-out times of new buildings, plaster surfaces have been replaced by plasterboard. Knock on the wall in different places to check if it is solid. A hollow sound is a good indication of a plasterboard surface and this requires special consideration.

✳ Fixings in Solid Walls

✔ In basic terms, a hole is drilled into the wall and a plastic or nylon wall plug is inserted. The item to be fixed is attached to the wall plug with a screw. For the fixing to be successful the three components – drill, plug and screw – must be matched. The masonry drill must be the correct size for the wall plug. If the hole is too small the wall plug will not fit and if it is too big the plug will turn and pull out when the screw is inserted.

✔ Each size of plug can usually be fitted with two sizes of screws. For example, a 6mm wall plug will take 4 and 5mm (No. 8 and No. 10) screws. In soft materials such as aerated concrete blocks it is good practice to use the larger size screw because this will cause the plug to push out further and give a better grip in the hole.

✔ Base units can be fitted to brick walls using common 6mm wall plugs and 4mm x 30mm screws. Wall units, however, must be fixed using at least 5mm (No. 10) screws and, to get the strength of fixing required, the screw must penetrate the brickwork by a minimum of 50mm. To achieve this, 8mm plugs must be used together with at least 5mm x 60mm screws. In aerated concrete blocks choose plugs that have side fins or an external thread designed to cut into the block and hold the plug in position.

✔ Normally a 6mm plug should be fitted into a hole made with a 6mm masonry bit. However, when drilling soft material such as aerated concrete blocks or plasterboard, there is a tendency for the sides of the hole to be a little powdery and this may spoil the grip of the plug. In these situations the grip can be improved by using a masonry bit half a size smaller than the plug: a 5.5mm bit for a 6mm plug.

Fixings in Hollow Walls

✔ There are three forms of construction where plasterboard is used: stud walls, timber frame and dry lining. The first two are similar in that the plasterboard is fixed to a timber frame. In modern houses the timber studs are spaced at 400mm centres but before metrification they were set at 18inches (450mm). It is worthwhile finding the studs because they will provide excellent fixings without the need for plugs.

✔ Most types of wall units are installed using wall plates that have three slots for the screws. When fixing these to plasterboard it is best to ignore the middle slot and rely on the two on the outside to avoid weakening the board.

✔ In the case of dry lining, plasterboard is stuck onto the wall with plaster dabs. The hidden wall is likely to be made of aerated concrete blocks. The dabs are randomly spaced out but, once again, if they coincide with a fixing they will provide a more robust anchor than a hollow wall fixing (use plugs suitable for aerated concrete blocks). Without the assistance of studs or dabs the strength of the fixing is wholly dependent on the condition of the plasterboard. If there is any damage in the vicinity the fixing will be weakened. The integrity of the board will also be compromised if holes are drilled close together.

LIGHT/MEDIUM DUTY FIXINGS

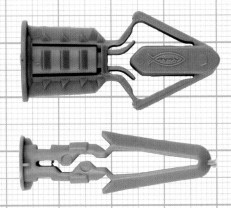

To make light/medium duty fixings there are special-purpose plastic plugs that have wings incorporated into the moulding. The plug is inserted into the drilled hole by compressing the wings between the fingers. When the wings reach the cavity they spring out and prevent the plug from being withdrawn.

NOTE If the house is a timber frame construction be careful not to damage the vapour barrier on the other side of the plasterboard. As soon as the bit has cut through the board relax the pressure on the drill.

MEDIUM/HEAVY DUTY FIXINGS

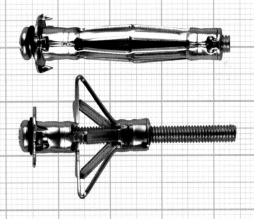

To fit wall units it is important to use medium/heavy duty fixings. Hollow wall anchors are suitable for this job. They are made of metal and have a machine screw fitted into a screw thread section at the end. When the screw is tightened it draws the threaded section towards the neck so that the four sides concertina out and grip the inside of the board.

NOTE In dry lining situations the insertion hole must be continued into the block; deep enough to enable the anchor to be inserted.

doit FIXING TO A DRY-LINED WALL

An alternative method for a dry-lined wall is to make a fixing into the masonry behind the board. Frame fixings fitted with screws (not hammer fixings) can be used in this situation. Although they are designed for fixing windows and doors, their heavy ribbing for use in aerated block make them suitable for dry lining.

1 To achieve a strong fixing the plug must penetrate the block by at least 50mm and therefore a frame fixing of at least 80mm will be needed. A hole of the same length as the fitting is drilled through the board and into the block behind.

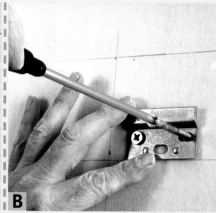

2 Remove the screw and tap in the plastic sheath as if it was an ordinary wall plug **A**.

3 Put the screw through the slot in the wall plate and insert it into the sheath **B**.

---

doit FIXING TO A STUD PARTITION

On stud partitions, if damage has occurred to the area where a wall plate must be fixed, use a wooden board to reinforce the plasterboard.

1 Choose an off-cut of board, preferably 18mm thick and large enough to span the damage **A**. In the area of the wall that will be concealed by the wall unit cut out a section of plasterboard large enough to pass the board through **B**.

2 Apply a generous amount of suitable adhesive **C**, insert the board and hold it against the back of the plasterboard whilst fixing the wall plate using ordinary wood screws **D**.

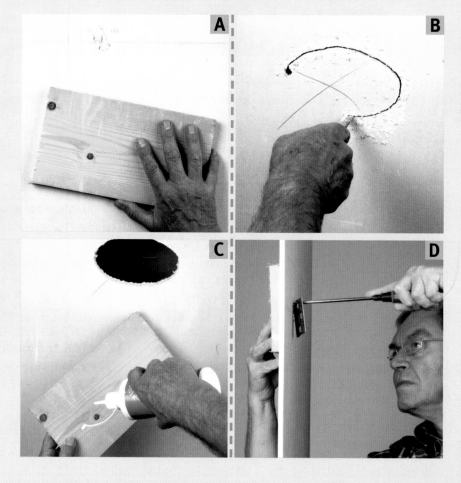

doit MAKE SPLIT BATTEN FIXINGS

Some wall cabinets are supplied without any means for fixing them to the wall – open display units, for example. The manufacturer may intend that they borrow their support from the cabinets on either side but there are situations when this will not be possible. The solution is to make a split batten fixing.

1 Take a piece of wooden board approximately 100 x 25mm and long enough to fit inside the cavity at the back of the wall unit **A**.

2 Cut the board down the length at an angle of about 30° (hence the name split batten) **B**.

3 Reassemble the batten, hold it in place in the back of the wall unit and measure the distance from the bottom of the batten to the top of the cabinet. Mark this distance on the wall **C**.

4 Fix one side of the batten to the back of the wall unit with its deepest side on the outside (towards the wall) **D**.

  Fix the other side piece on the wall with the bottom aligned with the line and the deepest side on the outside (facing the cabinet) **E**.

5 The wall unit is then fitted by simply hooking one side of the batten onto the other side **F**.

toptip*

To improve the stability on a stud wall, pack out the back of the unit where it straddles the timber framework. Insert a long screw from inside the cabinet, through the packing and into the stud.

Fillers

When the kitchen plan includes cabinets to be installed from wall to wall it would be unusual if it did not include fillers. Fillers provide the installer with some leeway to adjust the positioning of the cabinets and this could be essential, for example, when the walls are not square.

The front face of the filler will be on show and must therefore be cut from material that matches the trim colour as opposed to the general carcass colour. End support panels, decor panels and lengths of plinth or pelmet can all be used to make fillers (see below).

Another option is to use off-cuts of worktop material to make end fillers (see left) creating a wraparound effect.

KEEPING TRIM
The case study kitchens feature two types of filler. In the first kitchen *(top)* fillers have been made using worktop material. In the other kitchen *(right)* the fillers are end support panels that match the cabinet doors.

doit MAKE CABINET TO CABINET FILLERS

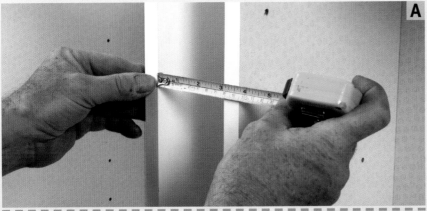

1 When the filler is to be inserted between two carcasses the long sides will be parallel because the edges of the carcasses will be vertical. Measure the distance between the carcasses and set this off from the factory-finished edge of the chosen material **A**.

2 Carefully cut along the waste side of the line. If there is a possibility of the saw ragging the face side, distance the saw-cut a couple of millimetres away then use a sharp plane to trim back to the line **B**.

3 Cut the filler to length.

4 The filler should fit snugly without distorting the cabinets. Fix it with screws through the carcasses at each side. Mark off the thickness of the filler on the inside of each carcass and drill three 4mm clearance holes through the centre line **C**.

5 Hold the filler in position using two clamps across the carcass gables and fix using 40mm x 4mm screws from each side **D**.

NOTE If the screw holes are drilled at the hinge or buffer position, as shown here, eventually they will be covered by the hinge and therefore hidden from view.

doit MAKE SCRIBED FILLERS

When a filler is used to bridge the gap between a cabinet and a wall additional work may be required. If the filler is wider than 50mm it may need to be fixed to the wall, so if the wall is out of plumb or has inconvenient bulges then you will need to make allowances.

The first task is to cut the filler so that it replicates the gap. If the wall is not vertical but is otherwise fairly flat then it may only be necessary to take accurate measurements at different heights, transfer these to the material to be used, then join them up to produce the cutting line. If, however, the wall is not so accommodating, then you will need to draw a line, representing the wall's profile, on the material. This can be accomplished using various methods, two of which are illustrated here.

Method A

1 The simple method is to hold the filler material against the wall in an upright position. If the floor is not level you may need to use a wedge.

2a The profile of the wall can be transferred to the material by running a small block of wood down the wall with a pencil held against it. The disadvantage is that this method may require three hands: one to hold the material, one to hold the block and the third to control the pencil **A**.

2b Using a compass instead of a guide block enables the job to be done by one person. One hand can hold the material whilst the other runs the compass down the wall. Particular care must be taken not to swivel or contract the compass **B**.

2c An ingenious but simple alternative is to use a round steel washer as a guide. The point of the pencil is held inside the hole whilst the outside edge is rolled down the wall **C**.

3 Once the material on the waste side of the line has been cut away the cut edge will be an exact replication of the wall profile **D**.

4 Although the filler will match the wall it will still have to be cut on the other side to fit against the edge of the cabinet. Hold it in place and mark the cabinet position on the backside of the filler at both the top and the bottom **E**.

Transfer these marks to the front side and draw a line between them to represent the cutting line.

5 Make the second lengthwise cut and then cut the filler to length **F**.

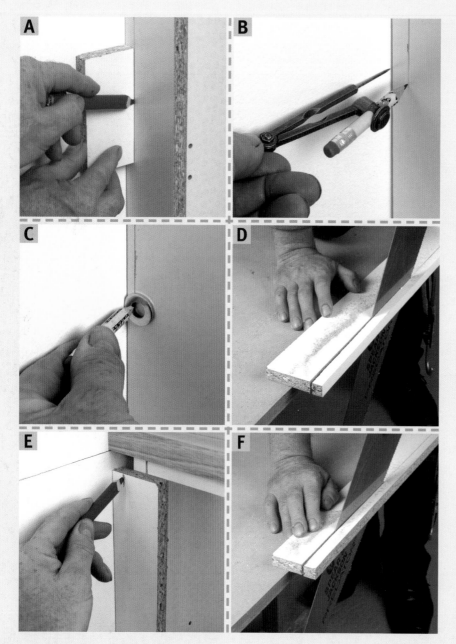

Method B

The drawback of Method A is that it does not take advantage of the factory-finished edge that is available on the raw material. This machined edge will be perfectly straight and square to the front side and can provide a virtually seamless continuation of the carcass.

To utilize the machined edge, the filler material must be set up against the cabinet with this edge perfectly plumb and therefore parallel to the gable of the carcass. The overlap (gable and material) must be the same as the guide used for drawing the line.

1 Assuming the distance to the wall does not vary by more than the thickness of the carcass gable, rough cut the filler material to the closest measurement plus the thickness of the gable. For example, suppose the gap is 50mm at the closest point and 60mm at the widest and the cabinets are manufactured from 15mm thick boards; the filler should be rough cut 50mm + 15mm = 65mm wide **A**.

2 Hold the filler material so that the machined edge is in line with the inside edge of the carcass. If it has been cut long enough to stand on the floor it should be possible to keep it in position temporarily using masking tape **B**.

3 Use a small off-cut of carcass board to act as a guide and draw a cutting line following the contour of the wall **C**.

4 When the filler has been cut to length it should be a perfect fit **D**.

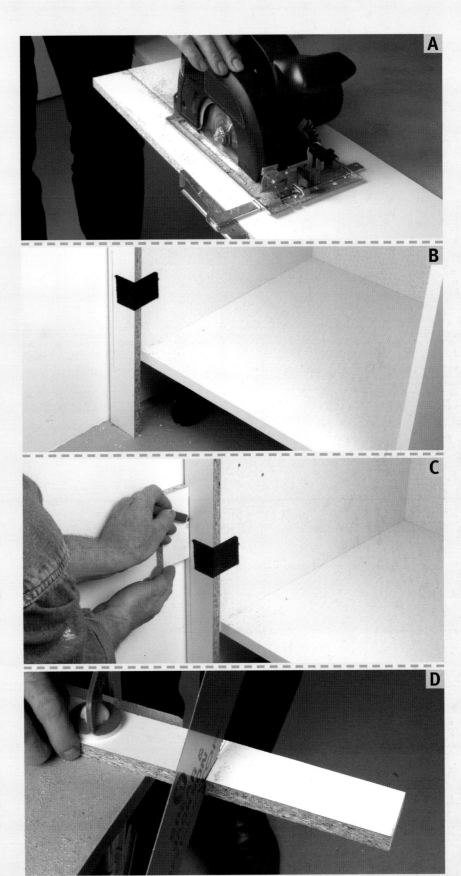

FIX THE FILLER TO THE WALL

For slim fillers, the screws that attach the filler to the carcass may be sufficient to hold it in place. Even so, it is sensible to run a bead of silicone down the wall where it will catch the back corner of the filler and help hold it in position. For wider fillers a more substantial form of fixing will be called for.

The best solution is to fit some form of batten down the wall behind the filler. Not only will this provide a firm hold on the filler but it will also add to the security of the adjacent cabinet. This is important if it is a tall unit.

1 Take a straightedge such as a spirit level or the machined edge of a board and, holding it across the carcass front, mark the wall at two or three different heights to represent the front edge of the fitted filler **A**.

Mark the top and bottom heights of the adjacent carcass to indicate the positioning of the filler. Using a straightedge draw a vertical line to join up the vertical marks **B**.

NOTE It will probably be necessary to remove the adjacent cabinet once the marks have been made in order to create working space.

2 Draw a parallel line down the wall set back from the marks by the thickness of the filler material. This will be the front edge of the batten **C**.

3 Cut the batten to length. It can be made from a piece of timber or spare carcass material. The length should be just short of the height of the adjacent cabinet.

4 Drill at least three 4mm clearance holes to take screws at the top, bottom and in between **D**.

5 Hold the batten in position: front edge against the line and at the correct height. Use a bradawl or a nail to mark through the holes onto the wall **E**.

6 Check the wall with the metal detector and if safe, drill 6mm holes at the marks. Plug the holes (see *Fixings*, page 94) and, making sure that the batten is the right way up, screw it to the wall **F**.

7 Fix the filler to the batten using stretcher plates, angle braces or furniture assembly joints **G**.

8 Refit the adjacent cabinet and join it to the filler with 40mm x 4mm screws through the gable as before **H**.

top tip*

If a batten is to be fitted in a vertical position mark the top with a T. Similarly, if fitted horizontally mark the right-hand end with an R. It is very easy to put the batten aside whilst the holes are being drilled and then to pick it up the wrong way round. If this happens the holes will not match up and the batten will be out of line. This simple indication will not only show the orientation but also the correct face.

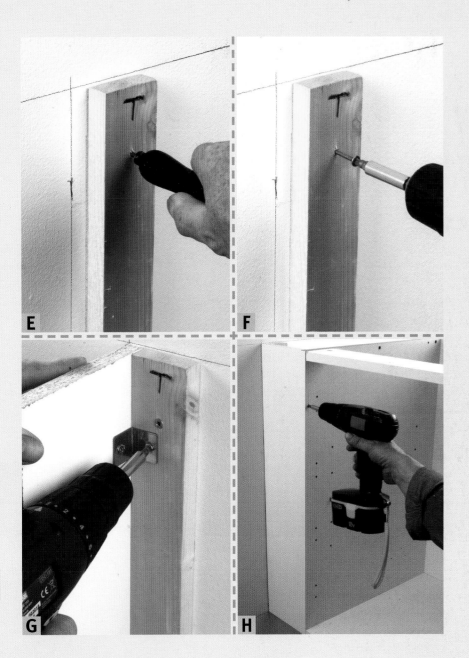

E

F

G

H

End Support and Decor Panels

Large panels are used for two basic purposes: support and/or cosmetic. If there is no base unit to support the worktop a panel can be fitted to take the weight and keep the worktop level. This can happen when appliances are put at the end of a run of units or where two appliances are next to each other.

The other use of panels is to cover exposed carcass gables and match them to the general trim colour. To reduce costs manufacturers tend to produce carcasses in the same basic colour throughout their range. The add-on panels transform a standard carcass into a particular style and the colour or finish can be matched to the door and drawer fronts.

SUPPORTING ROLE
There are various options for the finish of end support panels. Most common is a panel that matches the units *(above)*. If the worktop is a suitable material (such as wood, granite or stainless steel) then it can be used as an end panel *(right)*. This creates a stylish, wraparound effect.

The panels should be prepared so that the factory-finished edges align with the visible sides of the carcasses. When a panel has to be reduced in size the two cut sides should end up against the wall and the floor where they will not be seen. The following method will enable you to achieve this with the minimum of effort and at the same time produce a panel cut to the profile of the wall.

1 Stand the panel with the face side up against the gable of the base unit. Run a pencil line along the top of the base unit to mark the height onto the face of the panel **A**. Using a panel saw or a jigsaw with a down cutting blade cut along the line to remove the surplus.

2 Turn over the panel so that the cut edge is on the floor and the front face shows outwards **B**. The factory-finished edge will now be level with the top of the carcass and the forward edge will be vertical.

3 Measure the distance from the front of the carcass to the front edge of the panel and cut off a small piece to this length, less 2mm.
   Run this piece down the wall with a pencil held against it so that it scribes a line down the panel to match the profile of the wall **C**.

4 Saw down the waste side of the line. The panel should be a perfect fit **D**.

5 To attach the panel to the carcass, drill three or four 4mm clearance holes through the carcass gable, clamp the end panel in position and attach using 30mm long, 4mm screws.

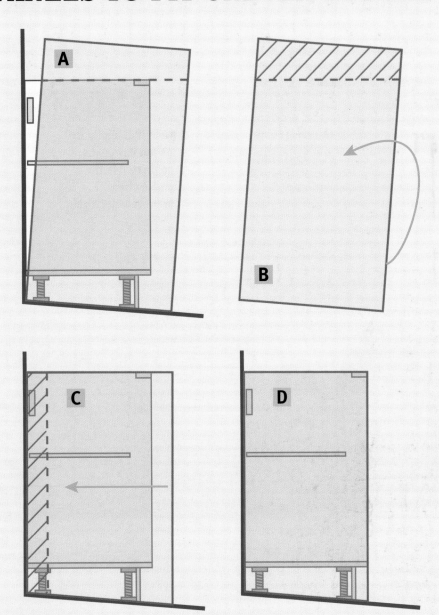

toptip*

The end panels supplied by some manufacturers are made to the standard height of the base units assuming that the floor is either perfectly level or that the unit datum line is set to the lowest level of the floor. However, they are wider than the base units and can therefore be scribed to the wall.

Second Fix Plumbing & Electrics

The electrician will need to complete the connections to the plug sockets and other accessories before the worktops go down and close the access to the rear cavity of the units. Once done the altered circuits should be tested to confirm that they are fault-free and within the safety margins. The electrician must issue a certificate (see pages 155–156).

top tip*

Note that appliances do not have to be connected to the circuits by an approved electrician.

The Kitchen Sink

There is a wide assortment of kitchen sinks to choose from. Not only are there different bowl sizes, shapes and combinations, but they also come in a variety of materials. The most popular type is the inset stainless steel, 1½ bowl sink, and although the fitting of other sinks may be slightly different the technique is similar.

The sink installation can be separated into the five basic stages, as outlined on pages 107–108.

Sink Options

Stainless Steel Inset

Inset sinks can usually be mounted either with the draining board on the right or left side. Good quality sinks incorporate a built-in seal to stop water penetrating the worktop.

Stainless Steel Corner

Corner sinks can be very useful in small kitchens with limited space. They are not recommended for laminate worktops because the sink cutout would weaken the worktop joint.

Round Inset & Drainer

These are designed to be mounted beneath hardwood or granite worktops. They are mounted in a board flush with the top of the cabinet. The board should be demountable in case the bowls need to be taken out after the worktop is installed.

Ceramic Undermount

Belfast sinks are mounted below the worktop on a short, purpose-built cabinet. Some flat-pack kitchen ranges may not include a special cabinet but as long as a short door 400/460mm high and 597mm wide is available, a 600 base unit can be modified to suit. Do not use with laminate worktops.

doit FIT THE KITCHEN SINK

Cabinet and Worktop Preparation

The first stage is to prepare the cutout for the sink and this must be done before the worktops are finally fixed. The cabinet below the sink may need some alterations. For example, if the front rail of the unit is fitted as intended (parallel to the worktop), it will protrude into the cutout area, as marked in pencil in picture **A**. It must be cut back **B**–**C** to enable the sink to fit properly **D**.

See pages 120–121 for making sink and hob cutouts.

toptip*

Mount the rail flush with the front of the cabinet to avoid having to cut away a sink aperture. This will maintain the strength of the cabinet.

Assembly of the Sink Components and Tap

It is much easier to attach the tap and clips before the sink is installed.

1 Fit the sink clips equidistant around the flange in the slots provided **A**.

2 The sink will have a 35mm hole for the tap on each side so that it can be installed as a right- or a left-hand drainer. Fit the blanking plate provided to the hole not in use **B**.

Continued on page 108

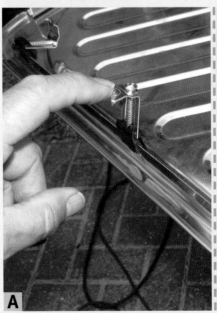

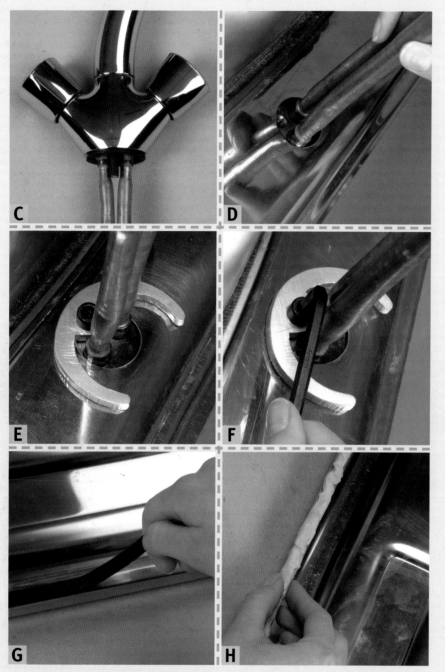

C

D

E

F

G

H

3 Many modern taps are monobloc – where both hot and cold water is delivered from one tap body. Screw in the threaded rod that is used to secure the tap and then the two copper pipes (tails) that will connect to the water supplies **C**. Finally, pass the rubber washer over the pipes and hold it against its seating position whilst the pipes are inserted through the hole in the sink **D**. Take care to ensure the washer does not move.

4 On the underside of the sink slide the horseshoe clamp over the tails so that the rod passes through the hole in the clamp and the arms of the clamp pass round the pipes **E**. Screw the nut onto the threaded rod and tighten the clamp against the underside of the sink **F**.

5 Usually, a foam rubber gasket is used to create a watertight seal between the sink and the worktop. The gasket has to be unrolled, the back tape peeled off and then stuck to the underside of the sink edge **G**.

Some manufacturers provide synthetic putty for this purpose. It has to be rolled between the hands into a sausage shape and applied to the edge of the cutout. When the sink is drawn down to the worktop by the clamps, the putty is squeezed against the sink to create the seal **H**.

If neither is included, make a seal using silicone sealant.

Connection of the Water Supply

1 Extend the hot and cold pipes until they are close to the tap position, terminated with couplings ready to accept the tails from the tap **A**. Alternatively, substitute tee junctions if supplies to wet appliances are required **B**.

2 The tails from the tap are made of soft copper and are reasonably easy to bend by hand. Gently bend the pipes into an upside down Y shape and adjust them to line up with the hot and cold supplies **C**. Over-manipulating them will cause damage.

NOTE Some Continental taps are fitted with 10mm tails and require an adaptor to convert them to 15mm.

3 Loose fit the sink into the cutout. Ensure that the sink clips can be clamped onto the underside of the worktop. Then line up the tap tails with the fitting on the end of the supply pipes **D**. Mark, then cut each tail leaving enough to fully locate into the supply fitting **E**.

4 Lift the sink and lower it in so that the tails engage in the fittings **F**.

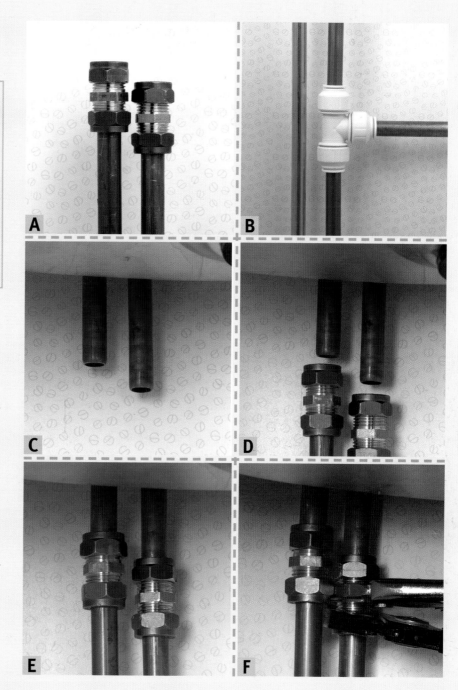

FLEXIBLE CONNECTORS

If the pipes are too far out of alignment with the tap ends use flexible connectors which can more easily be bent into shape.

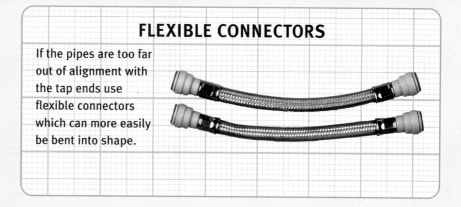

Connection of Waste

1 The sink waste fittings usually come in three main parts and are very easy to fit **A**. Apply a bead of silicone sealant around the edge of the hole and bed the top section into the sealant **B**. Insert the rubber gasket into the bowl of the waste and hold it against the underside of the hole with the overflow inlet correctly aligned. Insert the bolt and tighten with a screwdriver **C**. Wipe away any surplus sealant.

2 A 1½ bowl sink requires a special fitting that enables the two bowls to be connected to one trap. This fitting is made up of push-fit joints and pipes that have to be cut to size **D**. (See also *Fitting Waste Traps*, page 152.)

Use a piece of tissue paper to test the fitting for leaks.

Securing the Sink

1 The sink clamps **A** are hinged to allow them to be turned into position with the teeth under the worktop **B**. Sink manufacturers often insist that the screws are tightened in sequence to prevent the sink from developing a buckle.

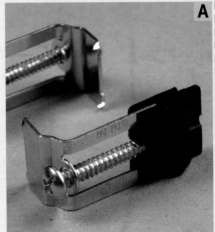

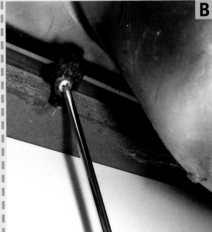

Washing Machines and Dishwashers

Modern washing machines and dishwashers only require a cold water supply but older washing machines need both hot and cold.

Special appliance valves are available that connect to the water supply with a compression joint (see *Anatomy of a Washing Machine Connection*, below). At the other end there is a 19mm screw-threaded socket for connecting the flexible hose from the machine. A red or a blue lever is fitted for turning off the supply. Fit a version that incorporates a non-return valve.

Provision for the waste should have been sorted at first-fix stage (see pages 77 and 78). The power supply for the appliance should be a plug socket fitted nearby, preferably in an adjacent cabinet where it is easily accessible (see also *Connecting Appliances*, page 164).

toptip*

The water hoses that are supplied with appliances are usually only 1.5m long. They can easily be swapped for 2.5m hoses if the machine is too far from the sink.

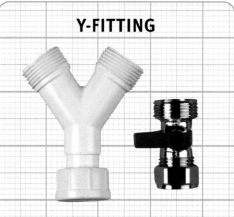

Y-FITTING

When a cold water supply is needed for a washing machine as well as a dishwasher, a Y piece can be fitted to the valve outlet to split the supply and avoid having to fit a second valve.

Anatomy of a **Washing Machine Connection**

If the washing machine and/or dishwasher can be located next to the kitchen sink it will be easier to connect to the services. The water supply can be taken from the hot and cold tap supplies and the waste can be discharged into a P-trap that incorporates a spigot inlet.

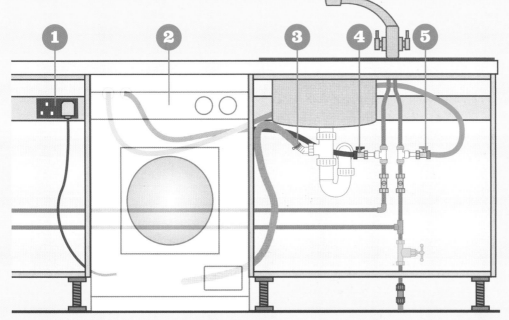

1 Power supply inside adjacent base cabinet

2 Washing machine

3 Waste pipe into P-trap spigot

4 Hot valve

5 Cold valve

Laminate Worktops

Probably the most widely used kitchen work surface is laminate. Available in a large range of finishes, they are cheap to buy and easy to maintain.

Standard laminate worktops are 600mm wide with a curved front side called a post-formed edge. Special versions are available with post-formed edges down two sides to use as a breakfast bar. A 900mm version of one of these can be fitted on a peninsular of base units leaving a 300mm overhang for the breakfast bar. The 600mm wide version can be fitted as a protrusion from the run, supported by a batten on the wall in line with the top of the base units and a central leg at the other end. The support leg and its socket should be fitted to the worktop before it is installed.

Worktops should not be left in storage too long because they are susceptible to changes in moisture. A local heat source such as a radiator or boiler can also be detrimental causing one side to expand and distort. Ideally they should be stored flat, in the original packing material, preferably in a similar environment to the finished kitchen.

WIDE APPEAL
A wider version of a natural stone effect worktop *(above left)* has been used to top an island of base units.

JOINT DECISION
Special corner strips *(above, top right)* are available in colours to match the laminate worktops. They are the quickest and easiest way to join two worktops together. A mason's mitre joint *(above, bottom right)* may take longer but will produce a more professional and hygienic finish.

Cutting and Joining

Laminate worktops require special treatment at corners so that they butt up together without leaving a gap. The simplest way is to use a special jointing strip *(above, top right)*. This is cut to length and screwed onto the cut end of the male worktop. When this is pushed up against the other worktop it will fill the gap and form a neat join. The disadvantage is that the joining strip will always be visible and may spoil the look of the kitchen. Apply clear silicone sealant in the join to make it waterproof.

Mason's Mitre

For a really professional finish the best solution is to make what is known as a butt and scribed joint or mason's mitre *(above, bottom right)*. Where the two worktops meet a 45° cut is taken through the post-formed edge and then parallel with the side. The worktop with the edge cut away is referred to as the female joint and the end of the other worktop, shaped to fit into this, is the male joint. When the two are brought together a near invisible join is created.

PLAN A WORKTOP CUTTING SEQUENCE

To avoid unnecessary wastage it is sometimes a good idea to work from a cutting plan showing where each section of worktop fits into the kitchen layout as well as the position of each join.

The diagram below is the worktop cutting plan for the kitchen on the right (not to scale). The dimensions marked relate to the lengths required before cutting to size.

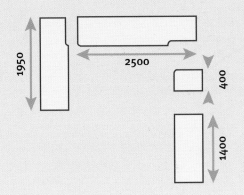

1950

2500

400

1400

Ways to Cut Laminate

3

HANDSAW When using a handsaw cut down into the laminate. Choose a 22in saw with at least 8 tpi (teeth per inch). Set the worktop securely on trestles, laminate side up and with the post-formed edge away from you. Cut down into the laminate and relax the pressure as the saw is drawn upwards. Try to keep the angle of the saw low on the down stroke.

CIRCULAR SAW An electric circular saw will do the job much more quickly and will maintain a constant right-angle cut. However, the cut must be made with the board upside down and the post-formed edge at the front; the exact opposite to the handsaw arrangement, because the blade revolves clockwise and cuts on the up stroke.

ROUTER For the best result use a router. When making cuts with a router the worktop can be either way up. The important point is that it should be used working from left to right and must cut into the post-formed edge and not out of it. Therefore the post-formed edge must be on the left-hand side at the start of the cut and to achieve this the worktop may have to be laid laminate side down.

✳ Cutting Laminate

✔ Cut the longest sections first. If a mistake occurs the long section will not be wasted because it can be utilized as a smaller section.

✔ Cut the joint end first and then cut the section to length.

✔ Cut the worktop starting at the post-formed edge.

✔ Cut and position the worktop that goes into the corner and has the female joint. The return section containing the male joint can only be measured accurately once the female section is in place.

✔ Follow the alignment of the front of the cabinets and not the walls.

✔ Make the cutouts for the sink and hob after the worktops have been mitred and loose fitted.

ROUTER JIG

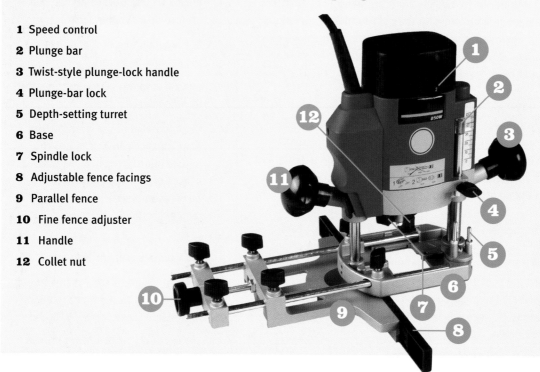

To cut a mason's mitre joint you will need to either buy or hire a heavy-duty router (see below) with a ½in (12.7mm) straight cutter and a special worktop router jig *(above)*. Several types of jig are available, so look for one that has the distinctive mason's mitre joint shape as well as holes to cut bolt slots with. These items are available to hire from good tool hire shops and cheaper worktop jigs are also specially made for the DIY market.

CAUTION ROUTER SAFETY

It is important to use ear defenders and goggles and to remove clothing that could get caught in the router. Always read and observe the instructions before starting work. These should include the following safety guidelines:

■ Make sure the work piece is firmly supported at each end. This means laying it on trestles or on a Workmate at the end being cut and a trestle of similar height at the other. They should be set out on firm level ground and the worktop should be clamped to the supports so that it does not move during the operation.

■ Make sure the cable will allow the router to move without dragging and will not come near the cutting area.

■ The cutter must be sharp. A cutter of less than professional quality is likely to lose its keen edge after two or three complete joints. The cut will then appear to be ragged.

■ Make sure the cutter is firmly held in the collet and that it remains absolutely perpendicular when the spindle is turned.

■ Make sure the guide bush is firmly attached to the router base plate.

Anatomy of a **Router**

For someone unfamiliar with a router some practice is advisable before attempting to cut the finished worktop. Most routers have largely the same key components. The following basic features are common to variable-speed plunge-base routers.

1 Speed control

2 Plunge bar

3 Twist-style plunge-lock handle

4 Plunge-bar lock

5 Depth-setting turret

6 Base

7 Spindle lock

8 Adjustable fence facings

9 Parallel fence

10 Fine fence adjuster

11 Handle

12 Collet nut

ALIGN THE WORKTOP

A worktop pushed back against an uneven wall may not be parallel to the front of the units and it is essential to maintain an even overhang to get a uniform appearance. It is not until the doors are fitted that a discrepancy will become apparent and by this time it will be too late.

The overhang will be the width of the standard worktop (usually 600mm) less the depth of a standard base unit (before the doors are fitted), which is usually 570mm, leaving 30mm for the overhang. This could be reduced to 25mm but generally a wider overhang looks better. One of the remedies below should be used to achieve an even overhang.

1 To make an assessment, temporarily lay the worktop on top of the cabinets and slide it over to the wall.

2 Measure the overhang at each end and adjust the alignment until it is parallel with the cabinet fronts and at least one part is touching the wall. Then consider the following:

A Is the overhang within acceptable limits (25 to 35mm)?

B Will any gap be hidden by the thickness of the wall tiles?

C If the worktop needs to go further back, can this be achieved by cutting out the high spots on the wall?

D Does the worktop need to be scribed to the wall?

It is much easier to cut out a high spot on the wall than to scribe and cut the worktop. As long as there are no hidden cables or pipes, a masonry wall can be cut back using a bolster chisel and a club hammer. If the wall surface is plasterboard a sharp knife will do the trick.

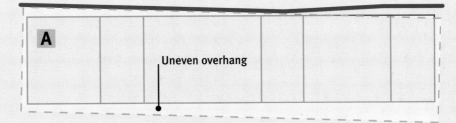

Uneven overhang

A high spot in the wall forces the worktop out of alignment

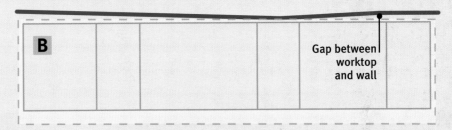

Gap between worktop and wall

Worktop straightened up at the front

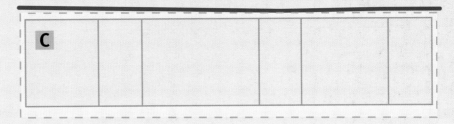

The high spot in the wall is cut back

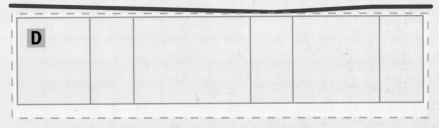

The worktop is scribed to the wall

Set up the Jig

There are several types of jig on the market and although they differ in detail they require a similar technique. They all have a central slot that acts as a guide for the router bush. One side of the slot is used for female joints and the other for male joints. One side of the jig is used for female joints and the other for male joints. They also have cutout guides for cutting the bolt slots.

Each jig is pre-drilled with a number of holes for inserting guide pegs. The holes used depend on the type of cut to be made and the width of the worktop. The pegs then act as length-stops for positioning the jig on the worktop.

Cut the Joint

1 The jig must be clamped securely with the pegs touching the worktop **A**. Check that the router can move smoothly along the whole length of the guide channel and is not impeded by the clamps.

2 Before switching on, set the depth stop. Place the router with the guide bush in the channel of the jig and lower the cutter until it touches the worktop surface. Temporarily apply the lock to hold the position whilst the depth stop is adjusted **B**. Wind the depth stop down to its full extent, then slacken it off by the depth of cut required and lock it there. Release the break to retract the cutter.

The first cut should not be more than 4mm deep to allow for the hard nature of the resin at the surface of the board. Subsequent cuts can be 8mm deep. If these depths are exceeded there is a danger of overworking the cutter.

3 With the guide bush in the channel of the jig and the cutter retracted, the router can be switched on. Never switch on the router with the cutter touching the surface.

4 Start the pass at the post-formed edge of the worktop **C**.

5 When the motor has reached maximum power start the cut. Plunge the cutter and apply the lock to hold the depth **D**.

---

top tip*

A professional kitchen fitter may be prepared to cut the mason's mitre joints for a fee. Indeed, in some areas there are tradesmen who specialize in this service exclusively.

Rules for Male and Female Joints

There are two rules that affect the way the joints are cut:

a) the router must travel from left to right (direction of routing must always be opposite to the rotation of the cutter) **A**.

b) the cut must start at the post-formed edge.

Consequently, in each complete male/female joint, one side will always have to be cut with the worktop upside down. Right-female and left-male joints are cut with the worktop laminate-side up **B**. Left-female and right-male joints, however, have to be cut with the worktop laminate-side down.

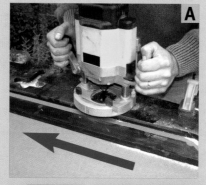

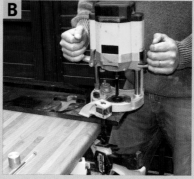

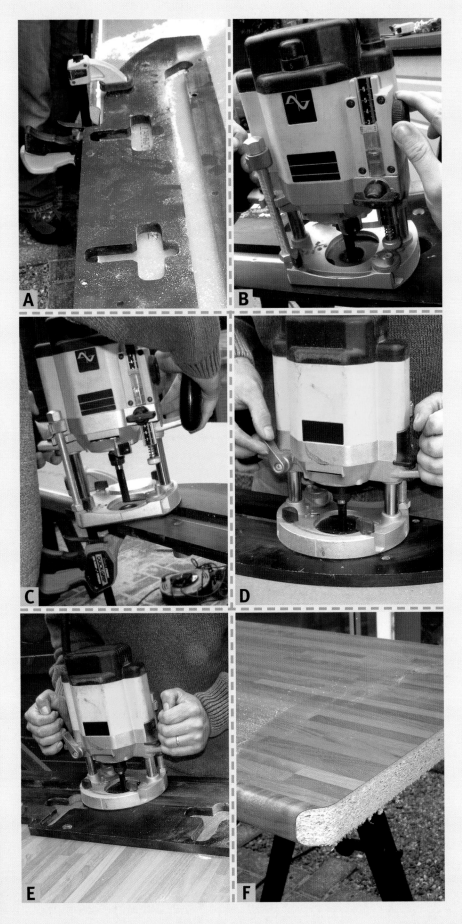

6 Move the router along the jig in an even motion; too fast can overload the motor and too slow may cause too much friction and scorch the work surface **E**.

7 At the end of each pass release the lock, switch off and wait until the cutter stops turning before readjusting the depth stop. (There is no need to take the router off the jig.)

8 On the final pass make sure that the guide bush runs smoothly along the far side of the slot in the jig.
There is a school of thought that advocates making all the initial cuts with the guide bush held against the near side of the slot and only using the far side for the final pass. The initial passes will remove the bulk of the waste and leave only about 1mm to be removed on the last cut when the cutter is fully extended.

9 Do not remove the router unless the cutter is retracted and has stopped turning.

10 Finish off with a light sand to remove board particles **F**.

do it   CUT BOLT SLOTS

1 Once the mason's mitre joint has been cut, reposition the jig on the underside of the worktop to cut the slots for the bolts **A**. Although two bolts, evenly spaced, will be sufficient to hold two 600mm worktops together, three bolts will make a better job.

2 The bolt slots on the female side must line up with the bolt slots on the male side so it is important to use the same measurements for both. Therefore mark the centre line on each side of the joint and position the middle slot over the mark **B**. Alternatively, set the first slot 150mm from the corner.

3 Cut the slots using the same technique as before, to a depth of between 22mm and 35mm **C**. The deeper depth will position the bolt in the centre of the board. Finish off with a light sand **D**.

WORKTOP BOLTS

Worktop joints are held together with special worktop bolts. They consist of two crescent-shaped flange plates with a bolt through the centre and an elongated nut on one end. Each pair of slots must be fitted with a bolt so that the flange plates pull on the shoulders of the slot to pull the joint together as the nut is tightened.

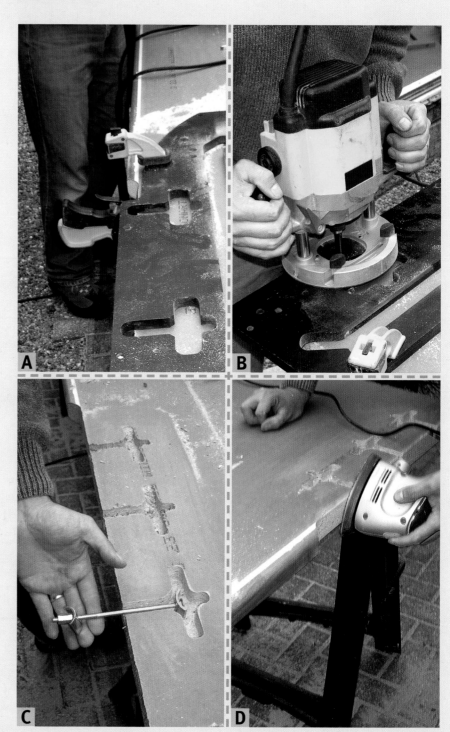

A

B

C

D

doit CUT TO LENGTH USING A ROUTER

If the end of the worktop is to be on display (either at the end of a run of cabinets or the end of a breakfast bar) use the router to get a perfect finish. Cut the worktop to length. The distance will be the length to the end of the run of base units plus the width of the overhang. Add an extra 5 or 6mm for trimming off with the router.

NOTE Use the same technique to make a male cut at an exact length.

1 Measure and mark the worktop for the length required. If a guide bush is fitted to the router and a jig is used to guide the cut, draw a second line set back 9mm from the first to allow for the offset created by the guide bush **A**.

2 Cut away the surplus worktop about 10mm from the line using a handsaw **B**.

3 Clamp the jig to the worktop so that there is a straight edge along the whole of the guide line **C**.

4 Trim back to the line using the router set to cut in small increments **D**.

5 Finish off by giving the board end a light sand.

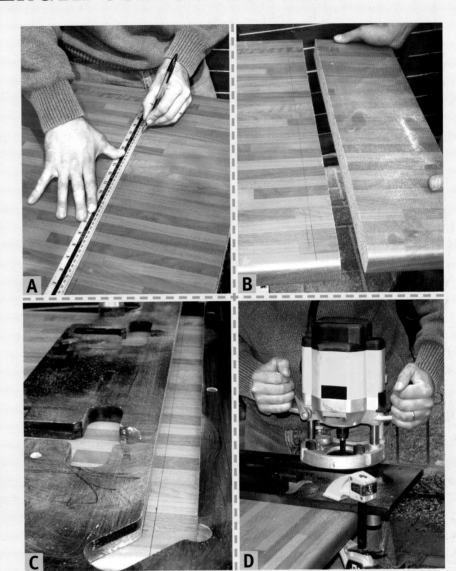

Cutting Angles and Curves

An angle cut or a curve is often applied to the end of a worktop to avoid having a sharp corner. In this case provide a wider overhang to allow for the return angle. On a breakfast bar make sure both corners are identical.

Some worktop jigs incorporate a graduated curve that can be used to create a swept end to the worktop. Set this up as before, but with a reasonable angle to the post-formed edge or it will be difficult to make a good job with the laminate cover strip.

toptip*

Use silicone carbide paper for sanding. It can be de-clogged by tapping it firmly.

The cutouts for the sink and the hob are done after the corners are mitred. The quickest way to make the cuts is to use a circular saw but it is easier (and safer) to use a jigsaw.

Ideally the jigsaw should have a power rating of over 700 watts in order to cut the laminate worktop and should be fitted with a downward cutting blade. Normal jigsaw blades are designed to cut on the up-stroke and may cause the laminate surface to chip.

NOTE The worktop must be fully supported on trestles before attempting the cut.

1 Place the worktop in position and, using a set square, transfer the width of the cabinet below onto the front edge of the worktop **A**.

Marking Up for a Hob

For a hob, divide the distance between the two marks to find the centre and extend this line across the worktop. To ensure the centre line is at a right angle measure from the end of the worktop. Use the centre line to set out the distances recommended by the manufacturer **B**.

Marking Up for a Sink

Sink packaging will probably contain a template that is useful but may not be appropriate for every circumstance. As a precaution, extend the two marks across the worktop to indicate the maximum extent where the bowl can be set without obstruction by one of the gables of the cabinet below.

In some cases the position of the sink bowl will govern the cutout. Here, the edge of the cutout must be worked out in reverse by measuring the distance between the bowl and the sink flange and setting this out from the line representing the gable.

toptip*

Make sure that the cutout section is supported during the cutting process. A clamp at each side may be all that is required. On wide worktops clamp a batten below. It is not until the off-cut falls on your toes that you come to realize just how heavy it is!

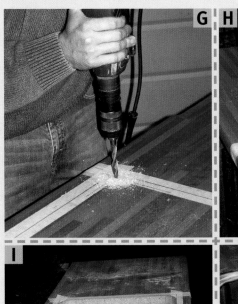

2 Lay the sink upside down on the worktop with the bowl inside the gable guide marks **C**. Use masking tape to mark the edge of the worktop with the flange at one end **D**.

3 From this mark draw a sideline parallel to the square end of the worktop **E**.

4 Set out the dimensions of the cut-out using the sideline as the starting point **F**. Drill a hole in each corner from which to start the cut **G**.

5 Do not engage the trigger until the blade is in the hole and the sole plate is on the surface **H**. Work slowly without putting undue pressure on the jigsaw (this causes the blade to bend and produce a slanted cut). Switch off before extracting the blade.

6 Carefully remove the off-cut piece and clean up the edges with sandpaper **I**. Check the cutout by inserting the sink **J**.

Sealing the Cut Ends

Wherever a cut is made in the worktop it must be sealed. The chipboard material that forms the core of the board is porous and, if it is unprotected, will soak up moisture, swell and raise the laminate surface. In this condition it is referred to as 'blown'. There are several products that can be used to seal the cut ends: polyurethane varnish, contact adhesive and silicone sealant are all suitable. Liquid types, such as varnish, require two coats to create a consistent moisture-proof barrier.

FIT LAMINATE END STRIPS

1 Worktops are usually supplied with a matching strip of laminate for covering exposed ends. Break off a section long enough to cover the end of the board.

2 Smear contact adhesive onto the laminate and to the exposed end **A**. Leave this to dry for about ten minutes. Only when the adhesive has formed a skin (when it is no longer sticky to touch) should the laminate be applied to the board.

3 Stick the laminate strip to the end of the board so that it overlaps the top by a few millimetres and most of the excess is underneath **B**. It will stick immediately and will not allow adjustments. Remove any surplus using electrician's side cutters **C**. It is important to press the laminate firmly. Use a small wooden roller, normally used to press down the edges of wallpaper. Or, hold a piece of hardwood against the laminate and hit it firmly with a hammer **D**.

4 The excess can be trimmed using a sharp, half-round fine tooth file **E**. Hold the file with both hands at about 60° to the edge and the handle slightly lower than the tip. Only engage with the laminate on the forward stroke and always cut towards the board. Finish with fine sandpaper to leave a slight bevel **F**.

top tip*

Pencil lines will not work at all on the protective film used on high gloss finishes. To overcome the problem, use masking tape. Simply stick down a length of tape and draw on top of it. The pencil marks will show clearly and the tape can be peeled off later without a trace.

METAL END CAP

Where the worktop butts up to a freestanding cooker, laminate edges could be affected by the heat. Use metal end caps on these edges instead.

doit INSTALL MITRED WORKTOPS

Just before the two worktops are joined, each face of the joint must be smeared with sealant. The primary function is to prevent the ingress of moisture but it also acts as glue. There are products available that claim to be specifically for this purpose but clear silicone sealant is difficult to beat.

The time available to tighten the bolts and adjust the joint is dependent on the setting time of the sealant and may be no longer than ten minutes. Consequently, it is important to be fully prepared before the sealant is applied.

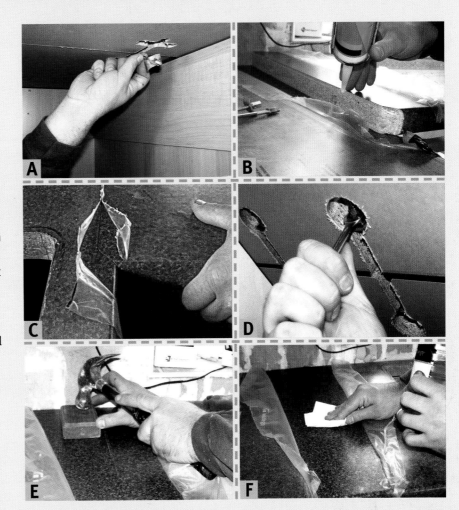

1 Make sure that the nut of each bolt is accessible. It is not unusual for the access to one side of the twin slots to be blocked by a gable of the cabinet below. In these cases, wedge the 'dead' end of the bolt in the inaccessible side of the slot and lift that section of worktop into position first. This will leave the other end containing the nut exposed but ready for the other section of worktop to be lowered on top.

If the slot is above a base unit with a solid top, such as a 900 x 900mm corner unit, an access hole must be cut out with a jigsaw.

2 Make a dummy run. Use a 10mm open spanner or an small adjustable spanner to tighten the nuts. Also have ready a hammer and an off-cut of wood. Bring both sides of the joint together and tighten up the bolts just enough to enable the exposed flange plate to engage with the shoulders of the slots. This will save time later **A**.

3 Apply a thin smear of sealant to the joint making sure that the surface edge is fully covered **B**. Lower the other side into position.

4 Move the worktops so that both sides of the joint come together and there is no gap at the post-formed edge corner **C**. Start to tighten the bolts. Work each bolt in rotation and continue until pressure is required to turn the nuts **D**.

Check the surface alignment before fully tightening.

5 If one side of the joint is proud of the other side try to force the high side down by thumping it with the side of a closed fist. If this is insufficient, put an off-cut of wood on the high side and tap this with a hammer **E**.

6 Fully tighten the bolts and check the joint again. Remove any excess sealant **F**.

7 Finally, the worktop can be fixed to the base units. Use 30mm x 4mm screws through the special purpose fittings used by the system: one screw per gable or pair of gables. In addition, fix the front top rails of the base units to the worktop.

toptip*

Use pieces of polystyrene foam saved from the packing materials to wedge the 'dead' end of the bolt into the hidden side of the slot.

Hardwood Worktops

Solid wood worktops are especially popular in traditional-style kitchens. They take a little more effort than laminate worktops, both at the installation stage and in terms of future maintenance (see page 131). They are also more expensive.

Hardwood worktops are commonly available as 3m-long timber blanks, 40mm thick and between 610 and 620mm wide. These timber blanks are supplied sanded to a fine finish on one side but untreated.

Timber worktops can also be purchased in a bespoke format, which are made up from a scale plan or from a customer's template. Not only will they be made to measure but they will be ready treated and can incorporate additional features (see pictures above). Some of these features would be extremely difficult to produce on site and mistakes could prove expensive.

NATURAL BEAUTY
Installing a beautiful hardwood work surface is not beyond the abilities of a DIY kitchen fitter. However, creating special features such as drainage grooves *(top left)*, inset hot rods *(bottom left)* and curved ends *(above right)* may be best left to the professionals.

If hardwood worktops are to be installed together with laminate worktops it may be important to note that they are 2mm thicker and wider than the standard 600mm.

Working with Hardwood

From the installer's point of view the dominant characteristic of hardwood worktops is their susceptibility to changes in humidity. The wood will always try to reach equilibrium with its environment: sometimes absorbing moisture and at other times drying out. The net result of this can be a change in dimension such that a 600mm wide worktop can shrink or swell by up to 4mm. Note that the effect is across the grain. The length will remain constant.

This width change presupposes that the change in humidity is the same on both sides of the board. When it is applied to one side only the board may warp. For example, if one side becomes too dry it will 'dish' (hollow); if too wet it will 'cup' (rise up). These effects must be taken into account when dealing with hardwood worktops. They must be protected from a local heat source such as a radiator and from moisture created by appliances such as a dishwasher. The air must be allowed to circulate on both sides and provision must be made for movement.

Case Study 1: A Reclaimed Hardwood Worktop

Recycled or reclaimed hardwood is an eco-friendly and affordable option for worktops. This piece of iroko, bought from a reclamation yard, was formerly a school science laboratory bench, complete with holes for a sink and bunsen burner! The owners want to sand it down and apply Danish oil to restore it to its former glory.

(Above) The worktop is cut to length using a circular saw, but could equally have been cut with a jigsaw or a router.

(Left) When a surface is covered in thick layers of varnish, use a scraper to get the worst of it off. Attempting to sand it first will only clog up the sanding sheets.

(Right) The owners chose a 750mm wide piece so that 10mm could be trimmed off to make an upstand. This was attached to the worktop with a biscuit jointer.

(Below) The grooves for the draining board were routed into the worktop using a special jig, available from DIY stores.

Extra Support

Hardwood worktops must be fully supported. Where an appliance is fitted between base units a batten should be fixed to the wall level with the tops of the units to act as a bearer. In addition, when two appliances are fitted next to each other a support panel should be installed between them so that the front of the worktop is supported down to the floor. Alternatively, a 40mm deep solid timber rail that spans between the units can be used.

Heat and Moisture Barrier

A special heat/moisture barrier must be fitted to the underside of the worktop where it passes over an appliance such as a washing machine, dishwasher, or microwave. This material is supplied in sheet form and is simply stapled to the underside of the worktop.

Worktop Layout

Hardwood worktops are usually a little wider than laminate boards. Although this is primarily to improve the finished appearance it does provide scope for scribing the backs to awkward walls. In addition, the worktop should be set forward to provide a 4–5mm expansion gap from the wall. A 610mm wide board will therefore overhang the base units by 15mm more than a standard laminate worktop.

top tip*

There is an old adage that was applied to the process of oiling worktops to protect them (see below): 'Once a day for a week, once a week for a month, and once a month for a year.' There is no doubt that the results would have been excellent for those who had time to wait.

doit HARDWOOD WORKTOP PREPARATION

Hardwood boards purchased as blanks must be treated with Danish oil. This will not make them waterproof, only water resistant. Two coats must be applied to both sides, and therefore they have to be treated before installation. End grain and cutouts should have five coats.

1 The first coat can be put on with a paintbrush: preferably a new one that will not add colour to the oil. Only apply as much oil as the wood will absorb **A**.

2 If the oil remains on the surface after about ten minutes wipe it off with a clean cotton rag **B**. Allow it to dry for at least an hour before putting on the second coat.

3 A light sand with fine sandpaper (150 grit) working with the grain can be beneficial between coats **C**. The first coat will have filled the grain and made the surface less absorbent, therefore on the next application be sparing. Never allow the oil to puddle on the surface. If surface oil dries, the wood will lose its attractive matt appearance. As a precaution apply subsequent coats with a cotton cloth.

A

B

C

✳ Rules for Installing Hardwood Worktops

CORNERS AND JOINTS

✔ Hardwood worktops must not be joined with a mason's mitre owing to the possibility of movement across the grain. Instead corners must be formed with a butt joint or a full mitre.

✔ On a join of 600mm or more it is recommended that three worktop bolts are used as well as four biscuits.

✔ On mitred joints the join should be reinforced with a metal or 9mm plywood plate. Screw the plate to the underside through oversized holes or slots aligned against the grain. Fix it using 4mm dome headed screws, separated from the plate with penny washers to allow for movement.

✔ Seal the end grain, including the bolt holes, with Cascamite wood glue and allow to dry before assembly.

✔ When the joint is put together, seal it as normal with clear silicone.

CUTOUTS FOR SINKS AND HOBS

✔ Set out the cutout for a sink or hob following the manufacturer's recommendation for sizes but check that the clearances will allow for cross grain timber movement. There must be a gap of at least 3mm front and back.

✔ The cutout must be no closer than 100mm from the end of the board or another cutout.

✔ Take the usual precautions when using machinery: no loose clothing; tie up long hair; always wear goggles and ear defenders.

INSTALLING BELFAST SINKS

✔ A quality one-piece cutout for a Belfast sink can only be achieved using a router and a jig specially made for the job *(above)*. Only attempt this if you are very confident using a router.

✔ For an exposed Belfast sink *(left)*, position it so that the front edge of the worktop is in line with the middle of the front wall of the sink.

✔ The worktop should overhang the back and side walls of the sink by 10mm. There must be a minimum distance of 300mm from the cutout to the end of the worktop.

✔ The worktop can also be installed in three pieces. It is cut and fitted on each side so that the worktop overlaps the sink walls by 10mm, then a reduced section for the taps is fitted along the back. The three sections are joined using worktop bolts. See top left picture on page 124.

Ways to Cut Timber Worktops

JIGSAW The hard nature and thickness of a timber worktop will test the power of a jigsaw. If this is the tool of choice use new blades, be patient with the cut and have spare blades available. There is no need to use down-cutting blades. Follow the same procedure as used for laminate worktops.

CIRCULAR SAW A more robust alternative to the jigsaw is an electric circular saw but the process requires care and strict adherence to safety rules.

ROUTER Forming the mitres and cutting the worktop to length can be done with a router. Cutouts for undermounted sinks and drainage grooves must also be made with a router and jig, although this is a difficult job and one perhaps best left to the experts. However, if the sink is circular the cutout should not be a problem because it is relatively easy to cut a circle with a router (see page 130).

RESIDUAL CURRENT DEVICE

When using power tools such as jigsaws, routers, planes and circular saws, use an extension lead fitted with an RCD (Residual Current Device). The extension lead will provide extra freedom and ensure that the cable does not drag and the RCD will protect against electric shock should the cable get caught in the machine.

Anatomy of a **Jigsaw**

1 Trigger latch
2 On/off trigger
3 Pendulum setting
4 Chip guard
5 Sole plate
6 Jigsaw blade
7 Dust port

CAUTION
USING A JIGSAW

■ As with any power tool, it is important to use ear defenders and goggles when using a jigsaw.
■ Remove any loose clothing that could get caught in the jigsaw.
■ Make sure the work piece is firmly supported so that it does not move during the operation.
■ Make sure the cable will allow the jigsaw to move without dragging and that it will not come near the blade while you are working.
■ Allow the machine to come to a rest before trying to draw out the blade.

CUTOUTS IN TIMBER WORKTOPS

1 Support the worktop on trestles so that it does not move about. Follow the same procedure used for laminate worktops (page 120) to mark out the cutting lines **A**.

2 Drill a hole in each corner large enough to insert the jigsaw blade and cut out the waste section **B**.

3 Do not engage the trigger until the blade is in the hole and the sole plate is on the surface **C**. Work slowly, without putting undue pressure on the jigsaw. Remember that hardwood is tougher than laminate. Cuts made in the direction of the grain require a lot of effort. It is important not to overexert the jigsaw.

4 Support the cutout section before completing the cuts into the corners.

5 Finish the cuts with sandpaper **D**. Treat with Cascamite resin wood glue, not silicone.

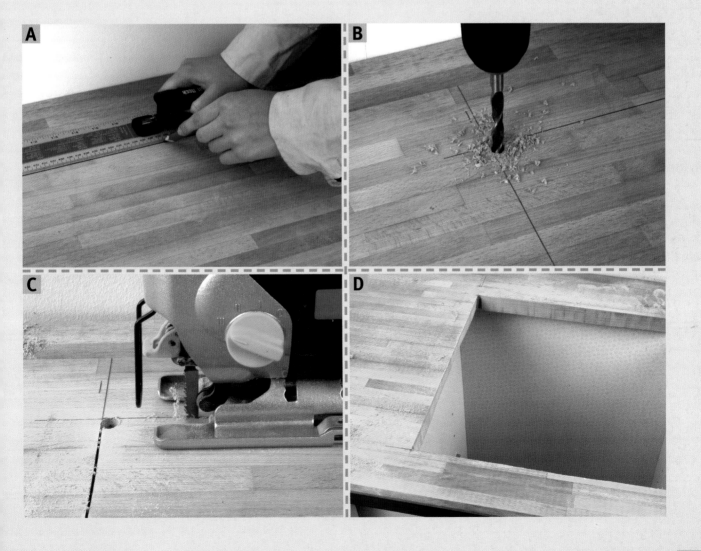

doit CUTOUTS FOR CIRCULAR SINKS

For a circular undermounted sink it is relatively easy to cut a circle in hardwood using a router. A simple trammel attached to the base plate will turn the router into a compass.

1 Measure the inside diameter of the sink and divide in two to get the radius. Subtract 7.5–10mm to allow for a worktop overhang. This will be the measurement from the edge of the cutter flute to the pivot point of the trammel and provide a guide to the size that it will need to be.

2 The trammel can be made from plywood or MDF and should be at least 6mm thick. Choose an off-cut as wide as the base plate of the router and long enough for the cut plus the base plate. Place the router on one end and mark the position **A**.

Use these marks to find the centre point and drill a hole 20 to 30mm for the cutter.

3 Attach the router to the trammel with the cutter in the approximate centre of the hole **B**.

4 Turn the cutter so that the flutes are in line with the pivot point and set off the distance measured at step one to arrive at the position of the pivot point. Drill a small hole just big enough for a round nail. In the upright position insert the nail and the trammel is complete **C**.

5 Stand the device on a wood off-cut, tap in the nail and practise the cut. The plunge distance on the router should be set to a few millimetres; just enough to mark a

circle. Plunge the router and swivel the trammel anti-clockwise. Check the outside distance against the circle required.

6 On the worktop mark the dead centre of the cutout for the sink **D**. Drive in the nail on the trammel.

7 Cut out the circle in increments of about 8mm taking care to move evenly and at a fairly low speed **E** and **F**. Do not stop or the wood will scorch.

8 Ideally the hole should be finished off with a chamfered top. This can be achieved with a suitable cutter with a pilot bearing wheel on the shank. Simply run the router round the cutout using the pilot wheel as a guide against the face of the cut.

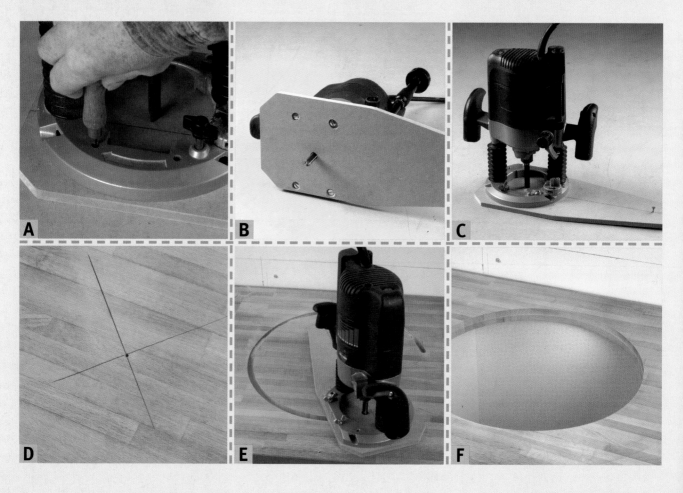

A

B

C

D

E

F

✳ Installing Hardwood Worktops

✔ Prior to installation cut a number of wedges from off-cuts of wood. These can then be inserted between the worktop and the wall to create a 4–5mm expansion gap.

✔ The worktop must be fixed to the base units with stretcher plates (see box, right); two per gable or pair of gables.

✔ If any of the base units have solid tops, at least 50% should be cut away to enable air to circulate.

✔ If the worktop is to be fixed to a solid top drill a 15mm hole and screw a penny washer over the hole.

STRETCHER PLATES

These brackets are screwed to the base units through the two screw holes so that the slots are uppermost for fixing to the worktop. Use 4mm x 30mm round head screws and fit one screw per stretcher plate only in the cross grain slot. The screw should be fully tightened and then slackened off a half turn to allow for movement of the worktop.

⑥ Ways to Treat and Maintain Hardwood Worktops

PROTECTIVE FINISH When you have completed the kitchen installation give the hardwood worktop another thin coat of Danish oil. It can then be left to dry undisturbed and free from dust.

LONG-TERM TREATMENT Further applications of oil are required throughout the life of the worktop to maintain its water repellency. If drops of water stop 'beading' on the surface, it is time for a fresh application. The areas around the sink are especially vulnerable.

MOP UP To maintain the worktop's appearance do not allow water to stand on the surface.

GENTLE CLEANING Only use clean water and a little washing-up liquid to clear away marks. Do not use chemical cleaning agents.

SAND DOWN Scratches and marks can be removed with fine sandpaper but this will also remove the moisture barrier so apply two or three coats of Danish oil afterwards.

SUN SENSITIVE Finally, the hardwood surface will be affected by sunlight. UV light will darken the wood so that if an object is left in the same place for some time a shadow effect will occur. Anything that is kept on the surfaces should be moved around regularly to avoid this.

Granite Worktops

To make an impressive design statement there is nothing to surpass granite. This luxurious material combines beauty with practicality: not only is it immensely hardwearing and heat resistant but used properly it can also give visually stunning results that will look good for many years to come.

On the downside, granite is expensive, brittle and very heavy. Cutting and polishing granite requires special machinery and the work can only be done in a dedicated workshop. Installing the worktop requires training and experience

POLISHED PERFECTION
Granite is the ultimate kitchen work surface. If the budget allows, use it as an end support panel *(above left)* for a luxurious finish. The granite worktop *(above right)* is a more complex installation, which requires a bespoke template – see the next page.

and although this may not be beyond someone with excellent DIY skills, it is best left to the specialists; if only because of the weight and fragility of the stone and the cost involved.

Preparation

Unfortunately, granite is prone to cracking. Some of the most beautiful varieties – those with large crystals – are particularly vulnerable. It is also much heavier than laminate or hardwood worktops. Consequently, it is important to make sure that the worktop is well supported.

Wall battens must be fixed around voids left in corners and across any appliance gaps left between base units. Extra care should be taken to ensure that the base cabinets are level, with all the legs properly extended so that the weight is evenly carried down to the floor.

Ideally, finish off the base units with a substrate (see *do it*, right) to strengthen the units and stabilize the granite.

toptip*

All types of stone, including granite, are porous and will need to be treated and maintained. Check that the supplier has impregnated the worktop with a sealant. Also, be aware that some manufacturers add various chemicals and dyes to achieve special effects in the stone.

Cutting a Template

For simple installations, such as a top for an island unit, a basic plan will be enough for the supplier to cut and dress the granite to. For more complex shapes, however, such as corners and cutouts, the granite should be prepared from a bespoke template. Usually these are cut from hardboard or thin plywood using simple carpentry techniques, well within the skill-set of a DIY enthusiast. However, it is very important to note that the person who makes the template carries the responsibility of any mistakes made in cutting out the granite. In consideration of the cost involved it is advisable to leave this job to the supplier, who will then carry the burden of correcting, and paying for, any mistakes.

Special Considerations

Narrow strips of granite at the front of hobs and some sinks are particularly susceptible to damage. It may only take a person to lean on a vulnerable section for the whole worktop to be spoilt. Make sure that the supplier reinforces these pieces, usually done by bonding a threaded steel bar into a groove on the underside. When using granite with large crystals it may even be advisable to ask the supplier for a spare.

 MAKE A PLYWOOD SUBSTRATE

The substrate should be made from 12mm plywood. It can either be let in to the top of each open unit and supported by battens **A**, or run across all the base units as a false worktop **B**. The granite can then be fitted to it using silicone sealant.

If the substrate is going to lie on top of the units, rather than be inset, keep it flush with the front of the units and allow for some form of cover strip to hide the edge of the plywood.

Granite slabs used for worktops are normally 30mm thick but 20mm thick slabs are also produced. These are generally used to form upstands, 65 or 90mm high. This is an important consideration where a granite surface abuts a different type of worktop such as hardwood or laminate. In these situations it is better to fit the substrate on top of the units so that the granite will lie slightly proud of the adjoining worktop **B**.

Sink, Taps and Hob

Undermounted sinks are a feature of granite worktops. Stainless steel and various china sinks, including Belfast sinks, can be fitted in advance of the granite installation. Although the taps and the hob cannot be installed until after the granite is fitted, suitable cutouts for them must be made in the substrate. A loose cutout is made allowing tolerance to adjust the sink in the granite. For a stainless steel sink use a router to cut a shoulder in the ply so that the rim of the sink sits flush with the top **B**. The sink can then be plumbed in.

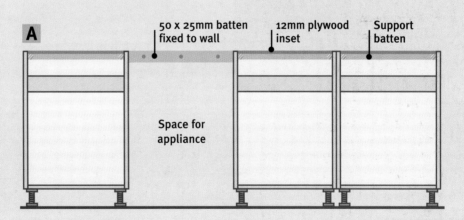

A — 50 x 25mm batten fixed to wall — 12mm plywood inset — Support batten — Space for appliance

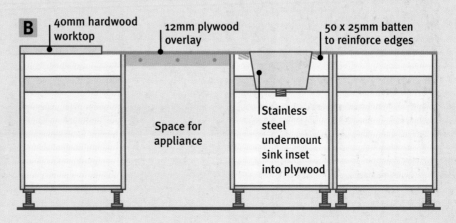

B — 40mm hardwood worktop — 12mm plywood overlay — 50 x 25mm batten to reinforce edges — Space for appliance — Stainless steel undermount sink inset into plywood

Pelmet, Cornice & Plinth

The pelmet, cornice and plinth are fitted to span the various units and create the illusion that there is one piece of furniture. The pelmet **A** and cornice **B** draw the wall units into alignment and add strength by spreading the load over adjacent units. They must be properly cut and fitted with neatly mitred joints and consistent overhangs. Any sloppiness will spoil the smart look of your kitchen.

All three are usually supplied in three metre lengths. If necessary, the plinth **C** can be cut to size using a handsaw but the pelmet and the cornice have to be mitred and this requires an accurate cut that can only be achieved with a mechanical saw.

MITRE SAW

The electric-powered mitre saw enables material to be cut quickly and accurately and can be mastered with very little practice. DIY-standard mitre saws are now quite affordable; fitting a kitchen may be the excuse needed to justify the investment. The mitre saw consists of a platform and fence with a very fine-toothed saw blade mounted in a frame that can rotate to angles between 45° and 90°. There will be preset stops at all the common angles. As well as the usual safety procedures for power tools there are additional precautions that apply (see right).

 Chopsaw Safety

✔ Make sure the blade guard is in perfect working order before the machine is plugged in.

✔ Keep both hands away from the blade area at all times.

✔ Do not attempt to cut exceptionally small pieces of wood.

✔ Raise the blade from the kerf before switching the chopsaw off.

doit USE A CHOPSAW

1 The chopsaw can be set up on a level floor or a firm workbench. The material being cut requires additional support on both sides and at the same height as the platform.

2 To make a right-angle cut, place the material on the platform with one side held against the fence. Bring the blade down without switching the motor on and adjust the material so that the blade will cut down the waste side of the mark. Hold the material tight against the fence and platform, check that fingers are well clear of the blade and make the cut.

3 To cut mitres requires a little additional planning especially when the material can only be cut from one side. A right-handed person would normally hold the material with the left hand and control the saw with the right hand. However, when there is insufficient material on the left side it would be necessary to change hands and hold the material on the right side. Not only does this feel awkward but it also adds a safety risk because some dexterity is required to control the handle, release the blade guard and operate the trigger. The design of some machines may in fact be biased towards right-hand use. To avoid this problem plan the cutting so that the awkward right side of the mitre (left end of the piece), is cut first, from the centre of a long length of material, leaving a fairly long off-cut to hold with the left hand.

4 As a general rule, when a piece has a mitre cut at one end and a right-angle cut at the other, cut the mitre first.

doit FIT THE PELMET

The pelmet is fitted to the underside of wall units and may be used to conceal strip lighting. It looks better if it is set back from the sides of the units by an overhang of between 12 and 18mm.

1 Take a set square and adjust it to the size of the overhang.

2 Mark the underside of the wall units at each corner from each face so that there is a cross to indicate the outside corner of the pelmet **A**.

3 Measure and record the distances from the wall to the cross or from cross to cross to find the length of each piece of pelmet **B**. It will be helpful to draw a rough sketch of the various pieces showing the cuts, with the lengths written against the outside face.

4 Working from the sketch, measure and mark each piece **C**.

5 The pelmet can be cut using a chopsaw or a mitre saw. Lower the blade without turning on the power and adjust the material along the fence so that the blade will cut down the waste side of the mark **D**.

6 Fit fixing blocks or angle brackets to the inside face every 600mm **E**.

7 Assemble each section using mitre adhesive specially made for this job. This is a two-part system. One side is lightly sprayed with the activator and left for a minute or two. **F**. Then a small amount of the glue is applied to the other side of the mitre in the form of a wiggly line. The two sides must be brought together immediately and held in position for about ten seconds for the bond to be made **G**.

8 Use clamps to secure each section in position under the wall units **H**. Attach using 4mm screws **I**.

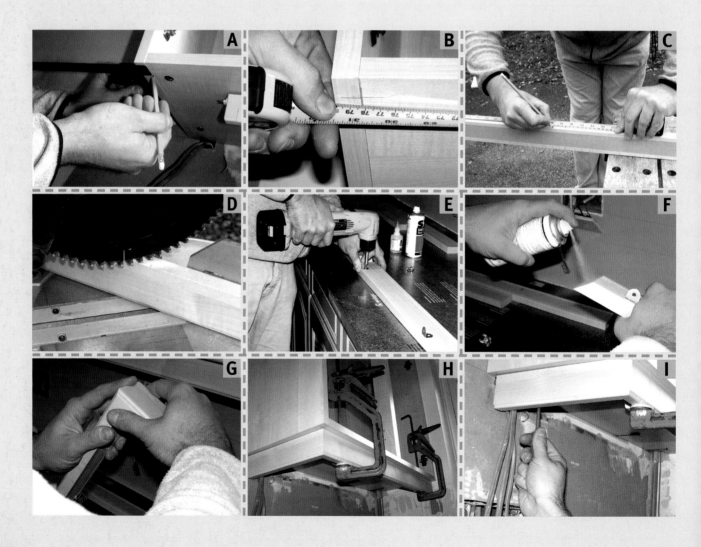

FIT THE CORNICE

The cornice has to be screw-fixed to the top edge of the wall units (plus any tall and dresser units). The cutting sizes for the individual lengths are worked out using a similar procedure for both the pelmet and the cornice.

1 The procedure is similar to the pelmet except that the back edge of the cornice is measured. The back of the mitre intersections are marked on top of the wall units using a set square. The set-back distance will depend on the style of the cornice but usually 20mm will suffice.

2 If a rough sketch is used to create a cutting list, mark the lengths on the back of each piece.

3 Use a chopsaw or a mitre saw to cut the cornice. When cutting the pieces that return to the wall, cut the mitre end first **A**. Then cut to length with the right-angle cut **B**.

4 Drill a series of clearance holes through the back tongue (the part hidden by the cabinet) before applying the mitre adhesive. Spray one side of the joint with the activator and wait until most has evaporated before applying the glue to the other side **C**. Immediately hold both sides together, forming the joint. **D**–**E**.

5 Place the assembled sections on top of the units and fix with screws (usually 4mm x 25mm) through the clearance holes **F**.

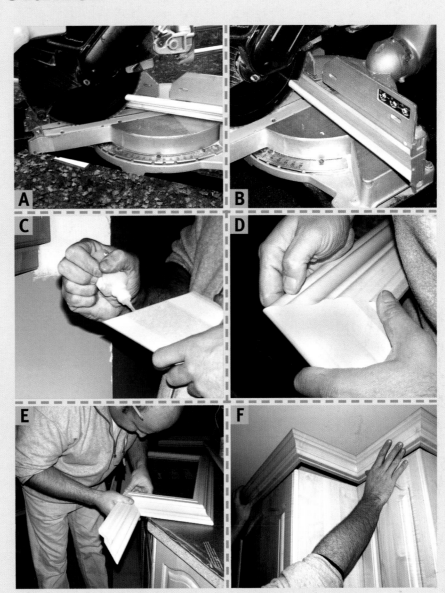

CAUTION
MITRE ADHESIVE

Care should be taken when using mitre adhesive. It is similar to superglue and the same precautions should be applied. It sets rapidly and if it gets on a finger do not touch another surface until it is dry.

toptip*

If there is insufficient room because of a low ceiling, the cornice can be attached from inside the units.

do it FIT THE PLINTH

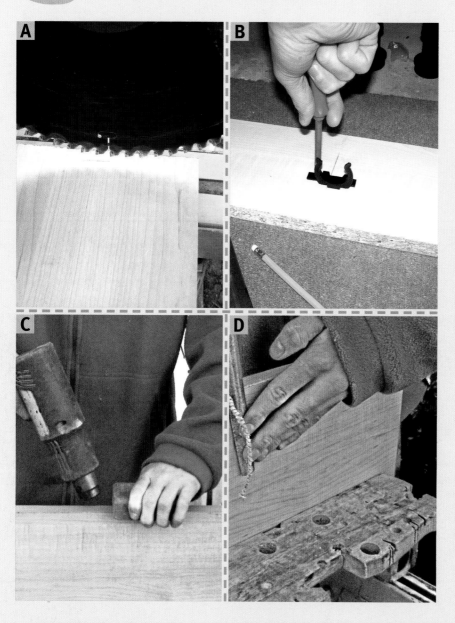

1 It may be easier to measure and cut the pieces one at a time **A**. On internal corners one length of plinth is cut oversized and fitted so that the excess runs beyond the corner, preferably as far as the next leg.

The adjoining piece is simply butted up to the first piece. On external corners, for example at the end of a run of units, the two pieces are butt joined, usually so that the front overlaps the side.

2 The spring clips used to attach the plinth to the cabinet legs are fixed to the back of the board with 3.5 x 16mm screws (see *Plinth Clips*, below) **B**. Mark the back of each piece with the position of the cabinet legs. Aim for a connection at least every metre. Fit the clips in the centre of the board but at an external corner, fit one low and the other high to enable them to clip onto the same corner leg.

3 To mask an exposed end at an external corner use iron-on tape, colour-matched to the plinth. It has an adhesive back that is activated by applying heat. Break off a length slightly over size, place it on the end of the plinth and hold a warm household iron on the surface until the glue melts. Alternatively, use a heat gun and press the tape onto the surface using a block of wood **C**.

4 After it has cooled and the glue has set, trim the surplus away using a fine file, in the direction of the board **D**.

PLINTH CLIPS

In all but the cheapest kitchen ranges the plinth is attached to the cabinet legs using plinth clips. Generally they are packed together with the legs and consist of two parts: the carrier that screws onto the back of the plinth board and the clip that slides onto the carrier.

Doors & Drawers

The final pieces of the jigsaw are the doors and drawers. If they had been installed earlier they would have obstructed the fitting of the pelmet and cornice. Now, as they are added the kitchen seems to come to life.

The development of kitchen door and drawer mechanisms is synonymous with an Austrian company called Blum. This company is credited with producing the first concealed furniture hinge in 1964 and this transformed the design of kitchen cabinets. Subsequently, their metal drawer runner system was used by many of the leading kitchen manufacturers. The company has driven technological advances in this field ever since.

CONCEALED HINGES

Concealed hinges consist of a mounting plate and the hinge itself. The hinge arm is manoeuvred so that the channel on the underside engages with a screw on the mounting plate. On the latest versions this is replaced by a clip mechanism that enables the door to be attached by operating a catch at the end of the arm.

doit FIT HINGES

1 In most cases the carcasses are predrilled with screw holes on each side for fitting the mounting plates **A**. When they are fixed to the carcass make sure they are on the correct side. The holes on the opposite side to the hinges are used for the plastic door buffers.

2 Doors are normally supplied with pre-drilled 35mm holes for fitting the hinges **B**. For the sake of efficiency, deal with all the hinges at the same time but do not fit the handles until the doors have been installed on the cabinets **C**.

toptip*

To ensure the hinges are properly aligned, insert both of them in the door and press a straightedge along the backs of both flange plates. Then mark the screw positions.

A

B

C

doit FIT HANDLES

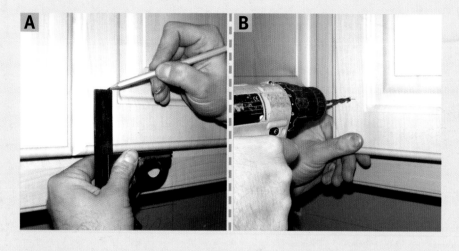

Fit the handles after the doors have been attached. Open the door before marking the handle's position; it is surprisingly easy to fit them on the hinge side by mistake!

1 The position of the handles is a matter of personal taste, but the positions must be identical. To achieve this, fit one handle and use it as the model for the others. Set an adjustable set square to copy the distance of the screw holes to the other doors **A**. Or, make up a template to copy the position of the holes onto the other doors.

2 When drilling the holes for the machine screws, use a sharp drill bit to avoid breakout on the back of the door. Alternatively, clamp an off-cut to the back **B**.

toptip*

If the machine screws supplied with the handles are too long they can be cut down using a strong pair of bullnose pliers or a small bolt-cropper.

doit ADJUST THE DOORS

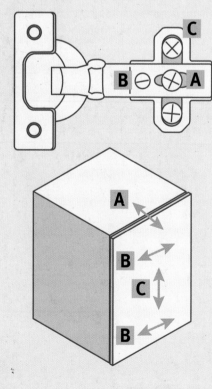

To achieve a smart-looking kitchen it is most important to adjust the doors and drawers so that they are all aligned to the same height and all the gaps are uniform. The hinge system enables the door to be adjusted in the following three different directions.

1 The door should spring shut and end up parallel with the carcass and resting on the buffers. If it does not close properly it is likely that one or both of the hinges has been set too close to the carcass. Loosen the mounting screw **A** and draw the hinge side of the door away from the carcass by a millimetre or so, then retighten the screw.

2 Sideways adjustments are made with the adjustment screw **B**. Turn the screws on both hinges to even up the gaps between the doors. To cure crooked doors, turn the screws on each hinge in opposite directions.

NOTE Sometimes it is necessary to slacken off the mounting screw in order to make this adjustment.

3 If necessary, the door height can be altered by loosening the screws on the hinge plates **C** and sliding the door up or down.

Drawers

There are several types of drawer system in common use and each one is fitted in a different way. Some are quite complicated, particularly the soft-close system, and therefore it is wise to allow plenty of time to deal with them. A set of four drawers can take up to two hours to install.

The job can be broken down into three distinct stages: the drawer runners, the drawer carcasses and the drawer fronts. It is not necessary to deal with all stages at the same time but if the job is split up be careful not to lose any of the parts from the open boxes.

doit CONSTRUCT AND FIT THE DRAWERS

1 Ideally the runners should be fitted before the worktops are installed. Most systems provide pilot holes ready for the fixing screws **A**.

2 It may be easier to understand the assembly of the drawer carcasses if the components are laid out in the front of you like an exploded view **B**.

3 Assemble the drawer carcasses on the workbench according to the manufacturer's instructions **C**.

4 Slide each carcass onto the runners.

5 To fit the drawer fronts, special brackets are usually attached and these in turn clip into the side panels of the drawer carcasses **D**.

6 The drawers are adjusted according to the manufacturer's instructions **E** and **F**. Normally the screws used for moving the front panel up or down form part of the clip-in mechanism.

7 If the drawers appear to lean check the alignment of the rails.

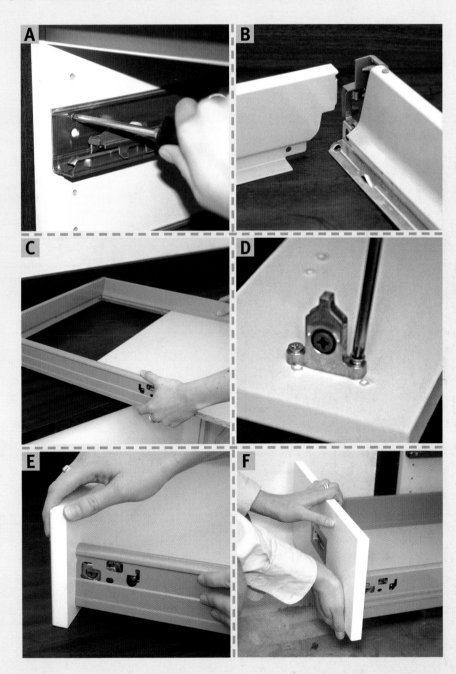

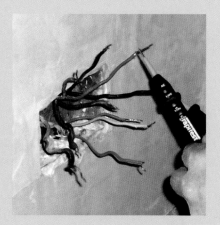

4

Plumbing Skills & Safe Electrics

Many DIY enthusiasts will confidently tackle
all manner of jobs around the home but are
reluctant to venture into plumbing and
electrical work for fear of making mistakes.
If this apprehension stems from lack of
knowledge then this chapter will tell you
everything you need to know.

Kitchen Plumbing

Modern materials and technological innovations have simplified home plumbing so much that any reasonably competent person can confidently tackle the majority of the work without having to call in an expensive professional. This is particularly true in the kitchen where the pipe runs are not complicated, no specialist skills are needed, and jobs can be accomplished with a few basic tools and techniques.

The tasks can be broken down into providing a water supply and taking away the waste. In the kitchen, the supply involves 15mm pipe and the waste 40mm pipe. Each has its own respective fittings and some of these have been made so user-friendly that all it takes to join them to the pipe is to push the two together. What could be easier than that?

✳ Forming Water Supply Pipe Runs

✔ Start by planning the main pipe runs; connecting the cold water from the stopcock to the rising main, and the hot water from the hot water cylinder to the sink tap position. Both pipes should be run parallel to each other but, of course, the water flow will be in opposite directions.

✔ Keep the runs to the corners of the room where they can be boxed in if necessary. If the horizontal runs are within 150mm of the floor they should not obstruct any of the appliances and it will avoid having to make cutouts at the back of the base units to fit over the pipes.

✔ Even the neatest pipework is not attractive so aim to make the runs as unobtrusive as possible. Set out the pipe clips using a spirit level to ensure that the pipes are horizontal or vertical, even though they may eventually be hidden behind kitchen units. Avoid diagonal pipework.

✔ Ideally, bends in copper pipe should be made using a pipe bending machine or a bending spring (see page 146). This will produce an easy bend that will assist the water flow. However, if neither device is available use an elbow fitting to make a 90° bend.

✔ Bends in plastic water pipe can be made using special formers. Alternatively, clip the pipe just before and after each bend. Do not reduce the radius to less than 8 x pipe diameter. Therefore the minimum bend for a 15mm plastic pipe has a radius of 120mm.

✔ Use equal tee fittings to branch off to feed wet appliances or an outside tap. Alternatively, this same fitting can be used to form a T-junction. Straight couplings are used to join pipe in line.

✔ If the pipework cannot be completed do not leave open ends. Either fit a push-fit stop-end that can be pulled off later when it is time to resume the run, or add an isolating valve. The pipe run can be continued, leaving the isolating valve in place.

✔ If it is necessary to take the run under a floor or through a ceiling, switch to plastic pipe. This can be threaded through awkward places, often in one continuous piece.

✔ Inadequately secured pipes can cause hammer noise. This may not be apparent until after the kitchen is fitted when it is too late. Therefore, make sure the pipes are fixed to the wall using pipe clips: 1m horizontal and 1.5m vertical for copper pipe but for plastic pipe reduce the spacing to 500mm horizontal and 1m vertical to stop the pipe sagging.

✔ If it is necessary to run a hot pipe behind a fridge or freezer, cover that section of pipe with lagging so that the heat does not affect the appliance.

✔ Make sure all joints are properly tested and watertight before they are covered over.

Anatomy of a **Domestic Plumbing System**

This diagram illustrates the indirect plumbing system found in the majority of houses. In some houses and flats, however, there may not be a storage cistern in the loft. Instead, all the cold water comes directly from the mains and the hot water is supplied directly from a combi-boiler rather than a hot water storage cylinder. It is always worth finding out exactly how the system in in your home is arranged before tackling any plumbing jobs.

1 Header tank
2 Soil stack vent pipe
3 Cold water cistern in loft
4 Gate valve
5 Hot water cylinder
6 Basin waste
7 Lavatory soil pipe
8 Bath waste
9 Soil stack pipe (SSP)
10 Washing machine
11 Rising main (shown in green)
12 Wall-mounted boiler
13 Dishwasher
14 Washing machine connections to hot and cold
15 Sink waste
16 Dishwasher connection to cold water
17 Outlet to main sewer

Key to pipes:
▬ = Rising main
▬ = Cold water
▬ = Hot water
➤ = Direction of flow

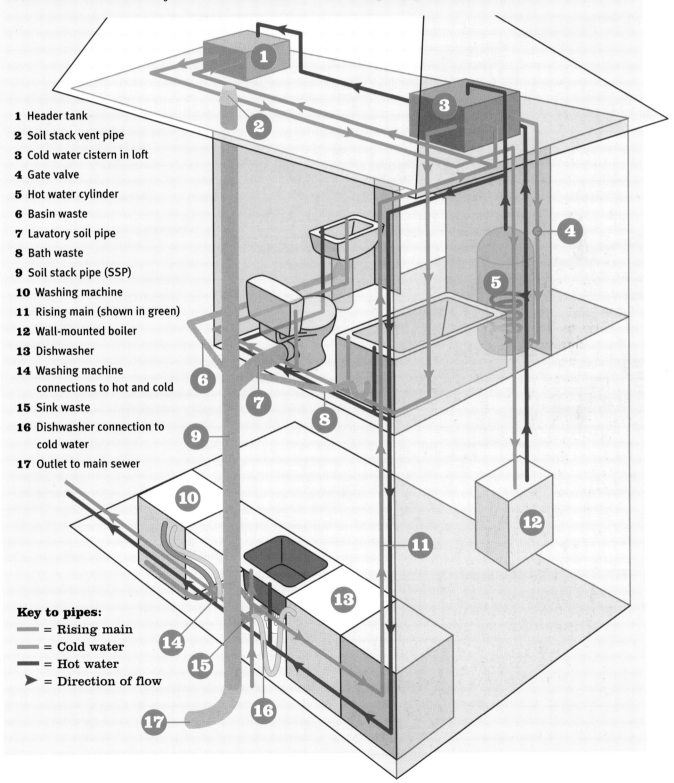

BASIC TOOLS AND MATERIALS FOR KITCHEN PLUMBING

The vast number of plumbing products that are available could easily deter a newcomer. Yet for kitchen work it is only necessary to deal with 15mm pipe and fittings for the water supply and 40mm plastic pipe and fittings for the waste. Nor do you need an extensive tool kit. Most plumbing work can be done using basic tools. More specialist tools are worth the investment if you intend to extend your new skills to other parts of the house.

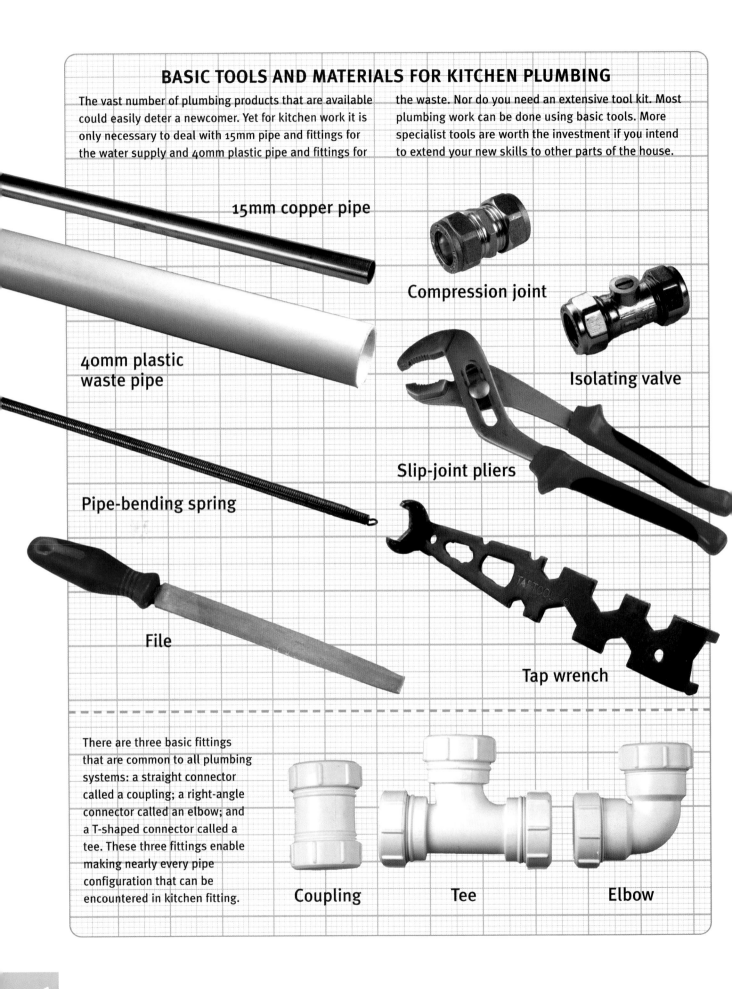

15mm copper pipe

Compression joint

40mm plastic waste pipe

Isolating valve

Pipe-bending spring

Slip-joint pliers

File

Tap wrench

There are three basic fittings that are common to all plumbing systems: a straight connector called a coupling; a right-angle connector called an elbow; and a T-shaped connector called a tee. These three fittings enable making nearly every pipe configuration that can be encountered in kitchen fitting.

Coupling

Tee

Elbow

Methods of Joining Supply Pipes

③

PUSH-FIT The easiest way to join pipes is to use push-fit fittings 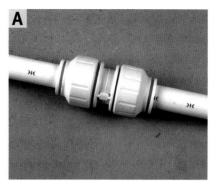. The pipe, either copper or plastic, must be cut square (see page 148). Each socket of the fitting contains a device that grabs the pipe and stops it pulling out. The market leader is the Speedfit brand. This uses a collet with stainless steel teeth to grab the pipe. The beauty of this system is that the pipe can be removed by depressing the collet at the mouth of the fitting, enabling it to be reused over and over again. The prepared pipe is pushed into the fitting (30mm) until it meets the stop-end. Although the pipe will not pull out, it is free to turn a full circle until the end-cap is tightened. This enables it to be lined up with other fittings and makes the job of assembling complex runs very easy.

COMPRESSION JOINTS Compression fittings are traditionally used on copper pipe but can also be used on plastic. They are found on fittings that may have to be removed for maintenance, such as isolating valves and washing machine valves. They are slightly more complicated than the push-fit systems as they need to be fitted with spanners **B** (see page 149).

SOLDERED JOINTS The traditional method of joining copper pipe is by making soldered joints. The fittings are neat and unobtrusive and if painted over are hardly noticeable. However, some practice is required in order to achieve good results. The joints are rigid and therefore do not forgive mistakes **C**. See page 151.

CHOOSING A PLUMBING SYSTEM

PUSH-FIT
Advantages Wide range of fittings available, including stopcocks and washing machine valves. Plastic pipe is useful to thread through awkward places. Easy to use; simple DIY skills only. Use with copper pipe to make inflexible pipe runs with a neater appearance. Easily undone, adjusted and reused.

Disadvantages Relatively expensive. Fittings are large and some are obtrusive. Most do not maintain earth continuity.

COMPRESSION
Advantages Readily available. Frequently encountered. Used on fitting that may need attention for maintenance purposes. Can be used on plastic pipe providing a pipe-insert is used. Can be undone and reused (with new olive).

Disadvantages Large and obtrusive. More expensive than soldered fittings. Need care when tightening.

SOLDERED JOINTS
Advantages Relatively inexpensive, especially end-feed fittings. Create a neat appearance. Rigid pipework.

Disadvantages Require special skills to apply. Danger from use of blow lamp. Cannot use on plastic pipe. Cannot be dismantled once it has been fitted.

doit CUT WATER PIPES

To make a successful joint it is essential that the pipe is cut squarely and properly prepared. The easiest way to cut pipe is to use a pipe-slice. All you need to do is simply place the pipe-slice on the pipe, slide it along to the cutting line and then rotate it until the wheel cuts through the copper **A**.

The result is a clean, square cut with a rounded edge.

A hacksaw can be used to cut all types of pipe but it does not leave a good finish. Copper pipe cut with a hacksaw must be deburred using steel wool and if it is to be used in conjunction with push-fit fittings,

any sharp edges must be filed away to avoid damage to the rubber O-ring that creates the watertight seal **B**.

Plastic pipe can be cut with a sharp knife **C** or by using shears designed for the job.

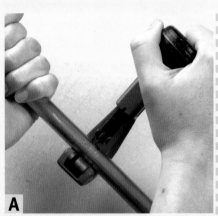

A

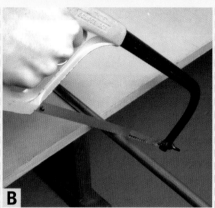

B

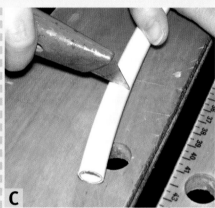

C

Anatomy of a **Compression Joint**

The diagram illustrates a straight coupling compression joint.

1 Copper pipe
2 Nut
3 Olive
4 Pipe end
5 Fitting body
6 Completed joint
  (shown reduced)

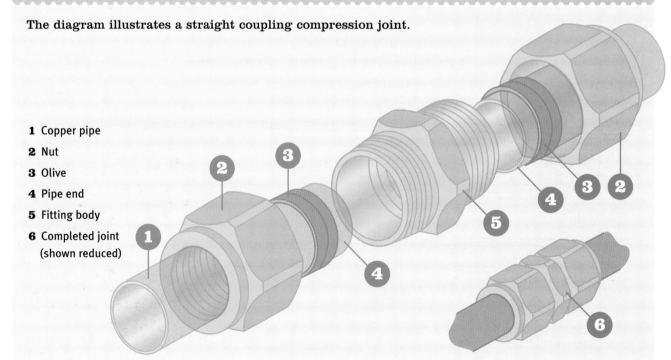

Planning and Fitting Kitchens

MAKE COMPRESSION JOINTS

1 Prepare the pipe as previously described (page 148) **A**.

2 Unscrew the coupling nut, remove the metal olive and check that it is smooth and undamaged. If necessary, rub it with steel wool **B**.

3 Slide the coupling nut onto the pipe followed by the olive, and push the pipe fully into the body of the fitting **C**.

4 Screw on the coupling nut as far as possible by hand. Then, using two spanners, hold the body of the fitting with one spanner whilst tightening the nut one complete turn with the other. Be aware that the joint may leak if it is not sufficiently tight or if it is over-tightened. If the joint does leak, give it a further quarter turn **D**.

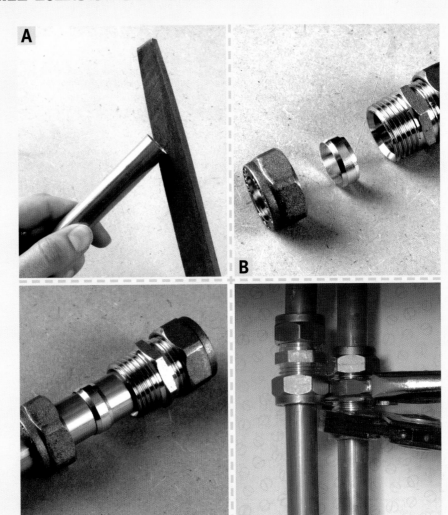

A

B

C

D

PTFE TAPE

A single turn of PTFE tape round the olive may help to ensure the joint is watertight.

CAUTION
TIGHTENING FITTINGS

When two compression fittings are in line it is particularly important to hold the body of the fitting steady whilst the coupling nut is tightened. If it is allowed to move, there is a danger that the other fitting will be slackened off.

Soldered Joints

Once a soldered joint has been made it becomes rigid. This can be an advantage, such as for connections to taps where movement would otherwise enable the tap to work loose. However, soldered joints leave little room for adjustment and the inexperienced person should consider that connections may have to be made inside cramped cabinets; this imposes the problem of using a flame inside an inflammable, confined space.

There are two ranges of fittings: end-feed and integral ring. Integral ring fittings already contain sufficient solder to make the joint but are double the cost of the end-feed fittings that require solder to be applied.

CAUTION SOLDERING JOINTS

■ Soldered joints work by capillary action and for this to happen it is essential that there is a close fit between the fitting and the pipe.

■ If the pipes in an older house are extended, the existing plumbing may be imperial and therefore cannot be soldered to metric pipes. The two sizes can be joined using compression or push-fit fittings, or adaptors are available.

■ Allow some time to practise the technique before you tackle the water supply.

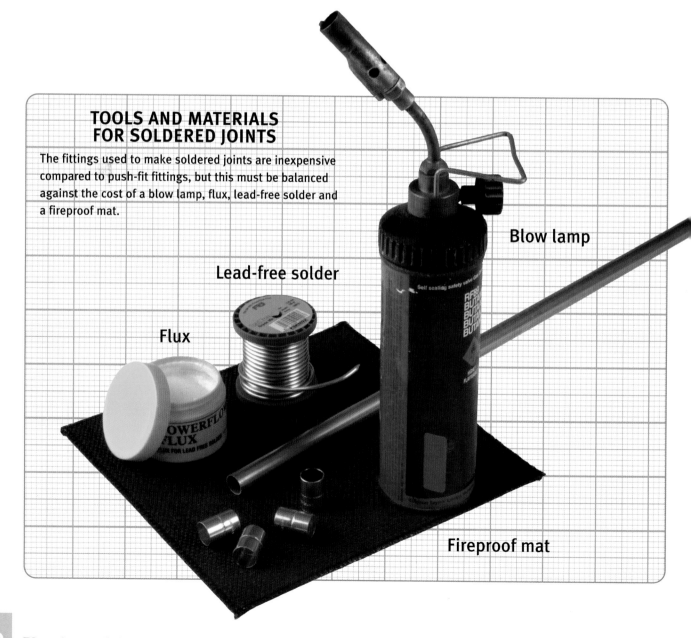

TOOLS AND MATERIALS FOR SOLDERED JOINTS

The fittings used to make soldered joints are inexpensive compared to push-fit fittings, but this must be balanced against the cost of a blow lamp, flux, lead-free solder and a fireproof mat.

Blow lamp

Lead-free solder

Flux

Fireproof mat

(do it) MAKE SOLDERED JOINTS

1 To achieve a successful joint it is essential that the copper pipe and the fitting be spotlessly clean. Use steel wool or fine emery paper until the metal is bright. It may be helpful to put the steel wool on the end of a pencil to clean inside the fitting **A**.

2 Smear flux on the cleaned surfaces to enable the solder to bond on the copper **B**.

Push the pipe into the fitting up to the internal pipe-stop, give the pipe a slight turn to ensure the flux is evenly spread, then wipe off any excess flux with a clean rag.

3a END-FEED FITTINGS
Using a blow lamp, apply heat evenly to the fitting until the flux begins to bubble **C**.

Remove the flame and touch the solder to two or three places at the mouth of the fitting. The solder should melt and be drawn up. When a bright silver ring of solder appears round the mouth of the fitting the joint is complete **D**.

3b INTEGRAL RING FITTINGS
All the joints have to be done at the same time because when heat is applied the solder at each end will melt. Apply the heat evenly over the whole fitting, not just the ends. Remove the heat as soon as bright rings of solder appear.

4 Wipe away any excess solder with steel wool and leave the joint to cool naturally for about 5 minutes **E**.

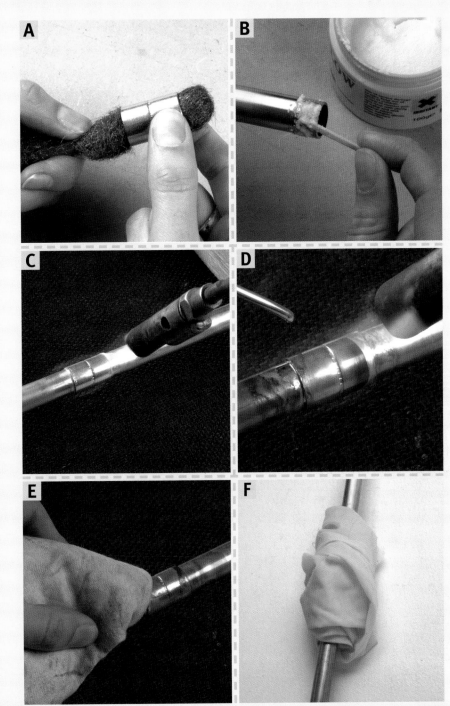

5 If it is not possible to make all the soldered joints at the same time on an end feed fitting, wrap a damp cloth round the joints already made. This will prevent the solder from melting when heat is applied to make the final joint **F**.

top tip*

If the solder runs down the pipe it is because the fitting was overheated. This will weaken the joint.

Waste Pipes and Traps

The waste pipe used in kitchens is usually 40mm diameter but must be increased to 50mm when the run is over 3m long. For maximum flexibility, choose solvent-weld pipe. This pipe can be used with all three types of fittings available for waste systems: solvent-weld, push-fit and compression. A similar-looking pipe made from polypropylene is unsuitable for solvent-weld connections.

Waste Traps

A trap must be installed between the waste pipes from sinks/wet appliances and drains. They are designed with a reservoir that traps water and this prevents smells from the drains filtering back. There are two basic forms: the P-trap and the S-trap, named after their shapes.

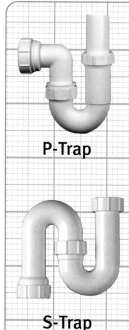

WASTE TRAPS

The P-trap has a horizontal outlet and should be used when the waste pipe enters the back panel under the sink. The S-trap has a vertical outlet and may be chosen when the waste pipe enters the sink unit from below.

There are versions of the P-trap that are particularly useful in kitchen fitting. For example, one type has an adjustable inlet that provides some flexibility in connecting to the sink waste and can also be converted to a standpipe trap by swapping the inlet spigot for a length of standard 40mm pipe. Another version has one (or two) spigots on the inlet for attaching the waste hose from a washing machine and/or a dishwasher (see page 78).

P-Trap

S-Trap

doit FIT WASTE PIPES

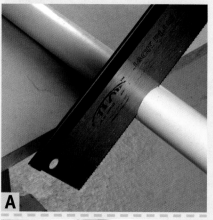

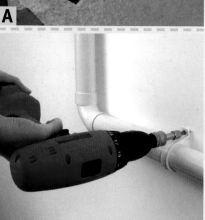

A

B

1 The pipe should be cut squarely using an old handsaw or a hacksaw and then smoothed with a file to remove the swarf. Use a rag to wipe away dust and filings. If the rough edge is not removed from inside the pipe, over time it will accumulate dirt and debris and reduce the flow **A**.

2 Fix the pipe to the wall using pipe straps at 500mm intervals and use 90° and 135° solvent weld fittings to change direction **B**.

toptip*

A simple way to indicate a square cutting line on a pipe is to wrap a sheet of paper round it so that the edge follows on round the pipe.

135° BEND

As well as the three basic shapes – couplings, elbows and tees – there is a useful 135° bend. All four are available as solvent-weld, push-fit and compression fittings.

doit MAKE SOLVENT-WELD WASTE JOINTS

These fittings are unobtrusive and relatively cheap but once fitted they cannot be dismantled. They are glued onto the pipe using a solvent cement that dissolves the mating surfaces. As the solvent evaporates, the surfaces weld together and become one. Check any instructions provided by the manufacturer, but generally proceed as follows.

1 Cut the pipe to length and smooth the ends **A**. In complex configurations, make up the pipe run first, without using the solvent.

2 Using a pencil draw a mark across each pipe/fitting junction to indicate the alignment and mark the depth of the socket on the pipe **B**. This will assist reconstruction.

3 Scour the end of the pipe and the inside of the socket **C**.

4 Paint a generous bead of solvent onto the pipe, push it firmly into the socket and give it a twist to spread the solvent and align the marks **D**. The joint will set within a few seconds.

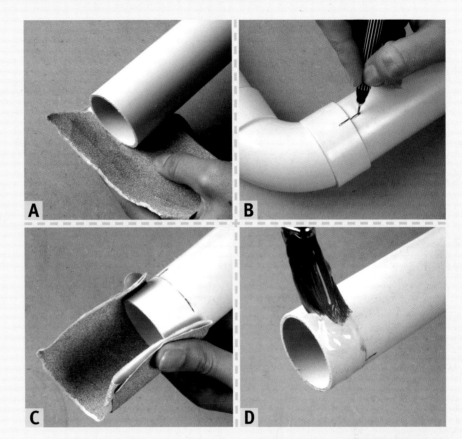

toptip*

Make sure the area is properly ventilated when using solvent cement and avoid breathing in the fumes.

doit MAKE PUSH-FIT WASTE JOINTS

Push-fit waste fittings have a captive rubber ring in each socket that seals the joint but enables the pipe to move. Lubricate the end of the pipe with a little silicone gel so that it slides in and does not dislodge the rubber seal **A**.

toptip*

When silicone lubricant is not available, use washing up liquid as a lubricant instead.

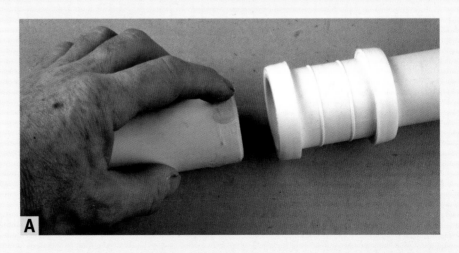

do it MAKE WASTE COMPRESSION JOINTS

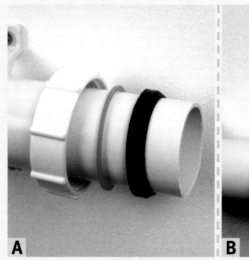

A

B

1 Remove the cap and slide it onto the pipe followed by the washer and then the rubber ring. If the rubber ring is tapered make sure the thin edge is towards the fitting **A**.

2 Place the pipe into the fitting and screw on the cap. As the cap is screwed onto the fitting the ring is squeezed against the pipe and the mouth of the socket to create a watertight seal. The cap should only be tightened by hand **B**.

do it FIT WASTE TRAPS

1 The inlet on the trap will have a ring that screws onto the waste outlet of the sink. Check the rubber washer inside and ensure that it is properly seated to make the watertight seal.

2 The connection rings only need to be tightened by hand. The use of a tool would create too much force that could distort the rubber ring and break the seal. Although the connection rings look similar there is no danger of the trap being installed

the wrong way round. The inlet will only connect to a sink waste outlet and is quite different from the compression joint at the trap outlet.

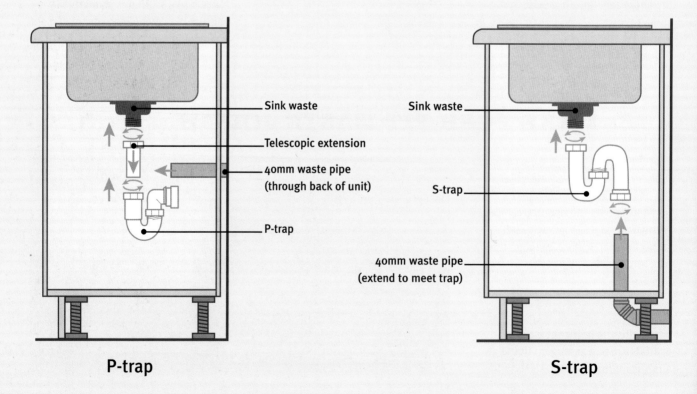

Sink waste

Telescopic extension

40mm waste pipe
(through back of unit)

P-trap

P-trap

Sink waste

S-trap

40mm waste pipe
(extend to meet trap)

S-trap

Kitchen Electrics

The Regulations

Safety standards for electrical installations have been in existence ever since 1882 but prior to 1st January, 2005, they were non-statutory. Someone carrying out electrical work did not need specific qualifications other than they should be a 'competent person'. On 1st January, 2005, everything changed when the Institution of Electrical Engineers (IEE) Wiring Regulations, the recognized industry standard, were incorporated into the Building Regulations. Henceforth domestic electrical work – both professional and DIY – came under statutory control and would be regulated under Part P (of Schedule 1 to the Building Regulations 2000).

The new regulations gain their teeth when it comes to selling the house. It is anticipated that solicitors acting for a purchaser will want to see the safety certificates. If they are unavailable it may jeopardize the sale.

The changes were introduced in order to raise the competence of electrical installers and make it harder for 'cowboy builders' to leave electrical installations in an unsafe condition, potentially leading to fires, injuries and even deaths.

Before work commences, the local authority Building Control Department must be informed of any electrical work to be undertaken in a kitchen, a bathroom or outside the house, as well as any major electrical work done elsewhere. 'Major work' might include installing a new circuit or changing a consumer unit. Building Control will charge a fee and inspect the work to make sure it complies with the regulations.

Electrical Work in a Kitchen

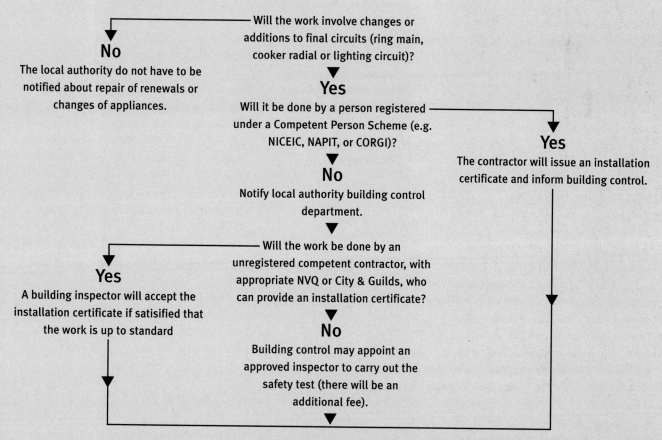

No
The local authority do not have to be notified about repair of renewals or changes of appliances.

Will the work involve changes or additions to final circuits (ring main, cooker radial or lighting circuit)?

Yes

Will it be done by a person registered under a Competent Person Scheme (e.g. NICEIC, NAPIT, or CORGI)?

Yes
The contractor will issue an installation certificate and inform building control.

No
Notify local authority building control department.

Yes
A building inspector will accept the installation certificate if satisfied that the work is up to standard

Will the work be done by an unregistered competent contractor, with appropriate NVQ or City & Guilds, who can provide an installation certificate?

No
Building control may appoint an approved inspector to carry out the safety test (there will be an additional fee).

Building Regulations (Part P) Completion Certificate

Using a Registered Installer

The new rules allow householders to by-pass the local authority providing they use an installer registered under the 'competent person scheme'. Contractors can become registered by demonstrating that their work meets the standards required in the IEE regulations. A registered contractor will give you a certificate confirming that their work complies with the regulations and will also notify the local authority.

These changes do not prevent householders undertaking electrical work themselves but it is essential to demonstrate that the work meets safety standards. The only way to prove this is to carry out a number of electrical tests that normally require specialist knowledge and equipment. This is usually beyond the reach of the average homeowner.

There is, however, another option. There are many competent electricians that have not registered under the scheme but are quite capable of carrying out all domestic electrical work, including the testing and issuing of certificates. The building inspector may be prepared to accept the work providing they are satisfied that it meets the requirements of the IEE Wiring Regulations (BS7671).

If the building inspector is not convinced he may bring in an electrical specialist to carry out the tests and this will entail an additional inspection charge.

What Can You Do Yourself?

Nevertheless, minor work can still be carried out by householders. The regulations only apply to fixed cables and equipment – the 'installation'. For work consisting of changing accessories and components, such as sockets and switches, or replacing a section of damaged cable, there is no requirement to inform the local authority. More extensive work done anywhere other than a kitchen, bathroom or outdoors is also excluded. For example, a competent person can add light points, sockets and fused spurs to existing circuits, and can install or upgrade bonding conductors (earth).

In the long run, it may save time and money to have the work done by a registered installer who is used to working within the regulations, rather than doing the work yourself. If you are in any doubt about your ability to carry out the work safely, you should always call in an expert.

Earthing

It is the nature of electricity that it will always try to complete a return circuit back to the supply company's transformer, taking the path of least resistance. Without a more suitable alternative it will use the earth itself. Someone who touches a live wire will receive a severe shock if the electricity is able to travel through their body to the ground.

The earthing system is an important safety feature because it provides a low resistance route for the electricity to take in the event of an electrical fault. It is made up of a network of conductors that link or 'bond' all metal pipes and appliances to the supply company's earth connection point near the meter. In rural areas the installation may be earthed using a large spike driven into the ground. Under fault conditions the earth network will carry a large current to earth quickly. This electrical surge will cause the fuse to blow (or the MCB to trip) and thereby disconnect the power and overcome the danger.

To conform with the latest regulations a 16mm earth cable should run from the supply company's connection point to a main earthing terminal block and then on to the earthing bar inside the consumer unit where all the earth cores (electricians refer to them as the Circuit Protective Conductors or CPC) from the installation cables are connected. The main earthing terminal block must be connected to all metal service pipes – typically water and gas but also any other structural metal parts such as oil pipes and air conditioning – using 10mm earth cables. Earth cables are identified by their yellow and green insulation and are perfectly safe to touch because in normal conditions they do not carry electricity. The regulations allow householders to carry out work on the earth system.

BASIC TOOLS AND MATERIALS FOR KITCHEN ELECTRICS

Although you may be dissuaded by the new regulations from carrying out major electrical work in the kitchen, Part P does not stop you from doing all electrical work. Adding a couple of specialist electrical tools to your kit need not cost much but will certainly make the work easier, quicker and neater. If you intend to do work on house circuits it will be essential to add a socket tester and a mains voltage indicator.

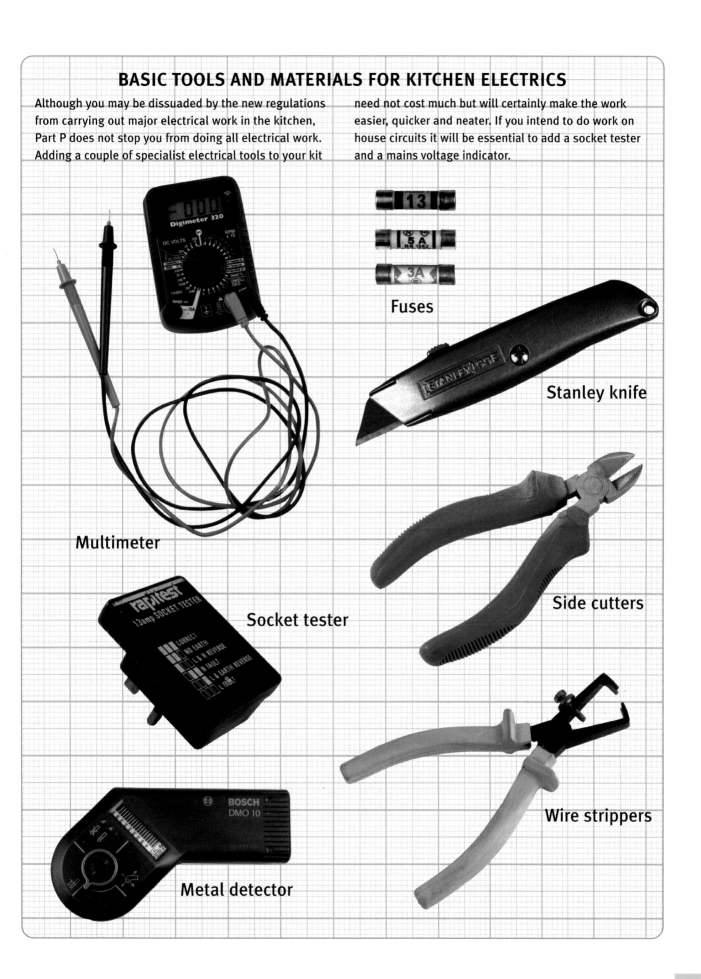

Fuses

Stanley knife

Multimeter

Socket tester

Side cutters

Wire strippers

Metal detector

Personal Safety

Many people steer clear of electrical work because of its technical nature and the fear that if they get it wrong there could be dire consequences. It is right to treat electricity with respect because slipshod work could cause injury and even fire. Yet of all the household jobs dealing with electricity is the least difficult. It does not involve the coordination skills required in areas such as carpentry and most domestic work can be accomplished with a few basic tools. What is essential, however, is a methodical, careful approach coupled with basic knowledge and guidance. When working on an electrical installation it is essential to pay attention to fundamental safety aspects. Most importantly, do not take chances. Do not assume the power is off without checking. If you have any doubts about the proposed work, the existing installation or your own competence, get help from a qualified electrician.

CAUTION ELECTRIC SHOCK

■ It is generally recognized that a current as low as 1/20th amp (50mA) can be lethal. This is about the same as the amount required to power a 10watt bulb.

■ An electric shock will occur when a person inadvertently becomes part of an electric circuit. The intensity of the shock will depend on circumstances such as humidity and insulation of clothing as well as age and fitness of the victim. A shock can range from a sharp tingling sensation to strong pulsations capable of throwing a person off a ladder.

■ Do not touch a shock victim before the power has been switched off or you too may become part of the same electric circuit. If this is not possible, stand on a dry object to insulate yourself from the ground and use something non-conductive, such as a broom, to separate the victim from the source of the shock.

■ Call an ambulance immediately. If the person is unconscious put them in the recovery position.

 SWITCH OFF THE POWER

1 Before any electrical work, the first thing to do should always be to switch off the power. Switch off the main switch on the consumer unit **A**.

2 Locate the fuse for the circuit on which you will be working and remove it **B**. Switch the consumer unit on again **C**.

toptip*

If MCBs (miniature circuit breakers) are fitted in place of rewireable fuses, tape the MCB switch in the off position to prevent someone inadvertently tuning it back on.

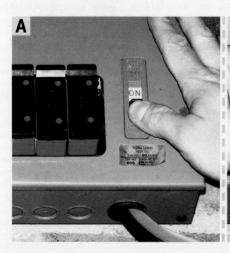

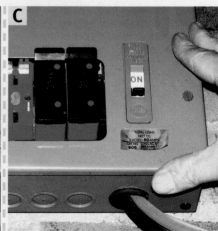

✔ **CHECK THE POWER IS OFF**
Before touching an exposed terminal or a bare wire, double check that it is dead by using an electronic mains voltage tester *(above)*. Test between positive and neutral and, if there is no response, test between positive and earth to confirm lack of power. Confirm that the tester is working by applying it to a live circuit before and again after the test.

✔ **ONLY USE PROPER MATERIALS AND FITTINGS**
Look for a British Standard number *(below)*. Check that cables and accessories are adequately rated and in good condition.

✔ **FIT THE CORRECT SIZE FUSE, FUSE WIRE OR MCB**
Fuses are a vital safety feature of an electrical system. If a fuse of a higher value is fitted it may not cut out if danger occurs (see also page 164).

✔ **USE GOOD WORKMANSHIP**
Make sure polarity is maintained. The positive (brown) and the negative (blue) must not be swapped over and must be connected to the specified terminals on electrical accessories. Use a socket tester to confirm the polarity. Make sure electrical terminals are screwed up tight, conductors are fully insulated, cables are correctly routed and protected, and that any work conforms to the regulations.

✔ **DOUBLE CHECK THE WORK BEFORE SWITCHING BACK ON**
Never be complacent.

✔ **WEAR RUBBER-SOLED SHOES**
This is an extra precaution to prevent severe shock because anyone can make a mistake. Similarly, do not work in damp conditions.

Anatomy of a **Domestic Electrical System**

Before you start working with electricity it is important to know how the system works. Electricity is measured in watts (W) and its flow (called the current) is measured in amps (A). It is distributed around the house on a number of different circuits. Each of these circuits is supplied by cables from the consumer unit or (in older installations) a fuse box. This controls the whole system and incorporates the main on/off switch as well as a MCB or fuse to protect each circuit. The usual electrical circuits encountered in the kitchen are described below.

■ Power

RING MAIN In modern systems a cable loops from the consumer unit to each socket or fused connection unit (FCU) in turn, then back to the same fuse at the consumer unit in the form of a ring. Power can flow from each side of the ring, thereby supplying double the normal current value of a single cable. The cable is 2.5mm twin and earth, protected by a 30amp fuse (or 32amp MCB). A ring main can supply an unlimited number of sockets and FCUs to a maximum load of about 7000watts, providing it does not serve a floor area of more than 100 square metres.

RADIAL When the floor area is no greater than 50 square metres the power circuit cable does not have to return to the consumer unit, but the circuit fuse at the consumer unit must be restricted to 20amps.

NOTE The maximum size appliance that may be connected to the power circuit (whether ring or radial) is 3kW.

- - - Ring Main Spur
One branch or 'spur' can be taken from the terminals of each socket to supply a new socket (see also page 164). Alternatively, the spur could be taken from a junction box wired into the ring main.

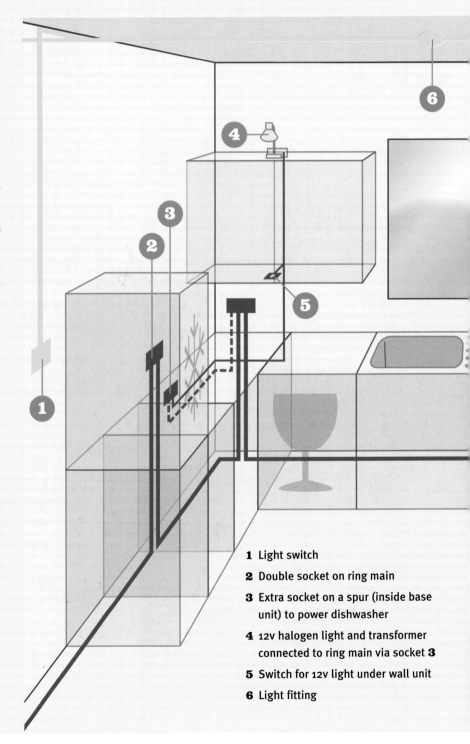

1 Light switch

2 Double socket on ring main

3 Extra socket on a spur (inside base unit) to power dishwasher

4 12v halogen light and transformer connected to ring main via socket **3**

5 Switch for 12v light under wall unit

6 Light fitting

The layout shown here is for a house with a suspended wood flooring with the cables running underneath it. In many modern houses the floor at ground level, where the kitchen is most likely to be, would be solid. In this case, the cables would come down from the ceiling.

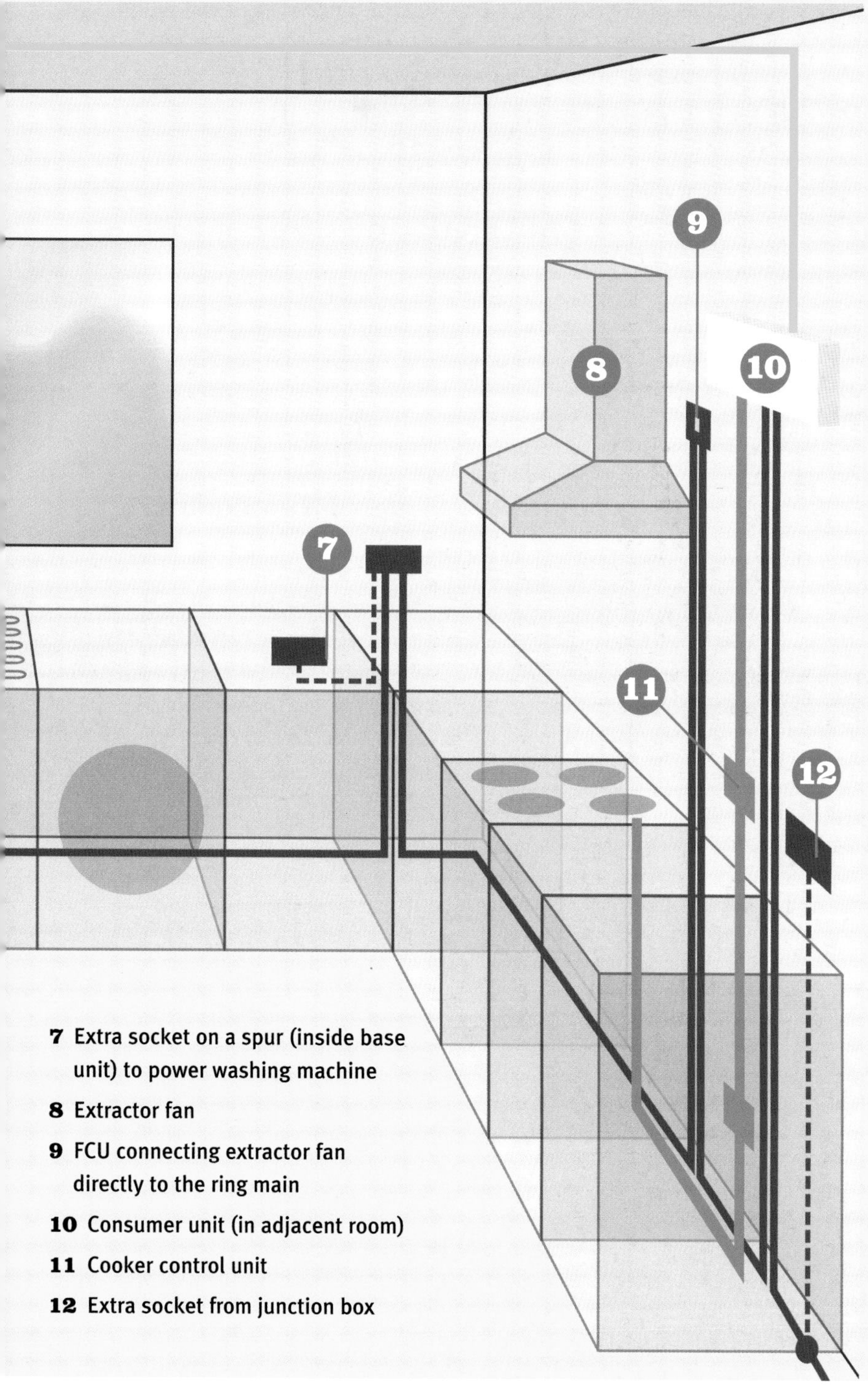

Lighting

One cable is looped from one lighting point to the next, usually with 1.5mm twin and earth cable. The circuit is protected by a 5amp fuse (6amp MCB) at the consumer unit.

FUSED CONNECTION UNIT (FCU)

An FCU that incorporates a switch can be used to connect kitchen appliances, such as an extractor fan, directly into the ring main without the need for a plug socket.

An FCU can be used to supply one or more sockets from the ring main providing the current demand does not exceed 13 amps and at least 1.5mm twin and earth is used as the spur cable.

Cooker Radial

A dedicated circuit is usually provided to any single appliance with a high current rating, typically the cooker. All-electric hobs and double ovens come within this category. Usually, 6mm twin and earth cable is used, protected by a 30amp fuse (32amp MCB) and this is normally adequate for appliances up to 17.6kW.

NOTE Single electric ovens (rated no more than 3kW) should be connected to the power circuit, but must be protected by a 13amp fuse.

7 Extra socket on a spur (inside base unit) to power washing machine

8 Extractor fan

9 FCU connecting extractor fan directly to the ring main

10 Consumer unit (in adjacent room)

11 Cooker control unit

12 Extra socket from junction box

Cable

The cables that are commonly installed in domestic premises incorporate two core conductors for positive and negative (referred to as phase and neutral) plus a third conductor for the earth (referred to as the circuit protective conductor or CPC).

Cable Sizes

Cables are normally referred to as 'twin and earth' (T&E) and have a size that relates to the cross-sectional area of the positive or the negative wires – the 'twin'. The thicker the core, the more current (amps) can be carried by the cable; the table below gives a reasonable indication. Actual current carrying capacity depends on a number of factors but is chiefly influenced by the method of installation. The values in the chart can be increased by an average 40% when the cables are surface mounted or decreased by 50% if they run through only 500mm of loft insulation.

CAUTION
CABLE SAFETY

Cable must be chosen to cope with the current demand of the circuit. If the capacity is inadequate the cable will overheat, causing premature aging of the insulation and become a source of potential danger.

FIXED AND FLEXIBLE CABLES

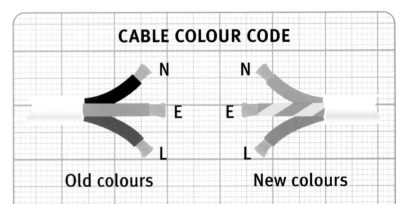

Fixed cable   Flexible cable

The flat, stiff cables *(left)* are intended for general house wiring (fixed), whereas the round flexible cables *(right)* are intended for connecting appliances to the power supply.

CABLE COLOUR CODE

Old colours   New colours

On 31st March 2004 the colours used to identify the core conductors of fixed cables were changed to be the same as those used for flexible cables – the positive red became brown, and the negative black became blue. All new installations after 1st April 2006 must be in the new 'harmonized' colours *(above right)*. The protective conductor, or 'earth', remains green and yellow. However, in flat cable, the protective conductor is left as a bare copper wire inside the outer PVC sheath.

EXAMPLES OF CABLE USE

USE IN KITCHEN	CROSS-SECTION[†]	CURRENT CARRYING CAPACITY
Lighting	1 mm	11.5 amp
Lighting and spurs	1.5 mm	14.5 amp
Plug sockets and FCUs (ring main)	2.5 mm	20 amp
Final connection to ovens	4 mm	26 amp
Cooker circuit	6 mm	32 amp
High-demand cooker/hob circuit	10 mm	44 amp

[†] cable enclosed in conduit in an insulated wall (e.g. aerated concrete block).

CAUTION HIDDEN CABLES

■ Hidden cables in walls are vulnerable to penetration by nails and screws. This could lead to a nasty electric shock or even a fire. To reduce the risk of such accidents the regulations specify the zones where cables can be concealed. Cables that are run within 50mm of the surface – wall, floor, or ceiling – must be protected by metal shielding such as a metal conduit. In walls, the regulations allow cables to be buried unprotected, providing they are run in so-called 'safe' zones described as follows *(shown in green on the diagram, right)*.

a) within 150mm of the top of the wall or partition.

b) within 150mm of the angle formed when two walls meet.

c) either horizontally or vertically to an electrical accessory such as a plug socket, switch or an FCU.

NOTE The zone in part c is extended to include the reverse side of a partition, 100mm thick, when the partition includes an opening – such as a door – that enables a person to reasonably determine the position of an accessory from the other side.

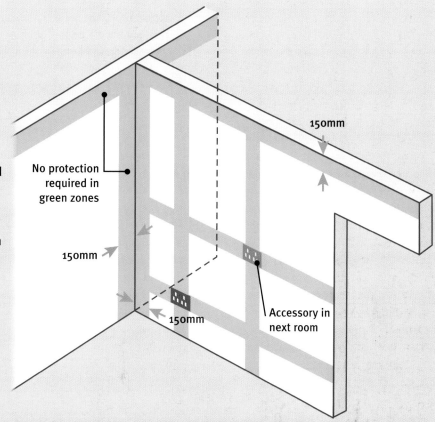

No protection required in green zones

150mm

150mm

150mm

Accessory in next room

■ Take care when working on an older house. Prior to the 1980s there was no specific requirement for cable routes in walls and therefore cables may be encountered in unusual places. In houses built in the 1970s, it was commonplace to run a diagonal cable from the cooker control to a cable outlet plate.

■ Cables should be kept away from hot pipes and separated from telephone wires by at least 50mm.

Connecting Appliances

Connecting appliances does not involve changes to the fixed wiring installation of the property and can therefore be done by a non-professional. Appliances rated below 3kW can be connected to the power supply (ring main or radial), either by a three-pin plug or by an FCU, fitted with the appropriate cartridge fuse (see right).

Cable should be connected inside accessories conforming to British Standards and these should be 'accessible for inspection, testing and maintenance'. Therefore, junction boxes should not be buried in a wall and plastered over and connection blocks (sometimes called 'chock-blocks'), are only acceptable if they are enclosed within a BS-rated box.

Appliances must have a 'suitably located' switch or plug socket so that they can be disconnected for maintenance purposes. This means that it should be fairly close to the appliance and reasonably accessible.

A power supply located behind an appliance is not acceptable unless there is an isolation switch located where it can be reached without having to move something out of the way. A plug socket placed in an adjacent base unit where it will not be obscured by the contents will comply, but one placed behind a drawer will not.

CAUTION USE THE RIGHT FUSE

It is important to choose the correct cartridge fuse for the appliance's power. Check the appliance to find its wattage (power). Then simply divide this number by 230 (the voltage) to find the current required (amps).

For example, a single oven may be rated at 2900 watts, therefore:

$$2900 \text{ watts} \div 230 \text{ volts} = 12.61 \text{ amps}$$

In this case a 13amp fuse should be fitted.

 ## ADD SOCKETS TO THE RING MAIN

A good way to add extra power outlets for appliances is to break the ring main and create a loop that links surface-mounted plug sockets fitted high up in the base units.

In the example below, the circuit link between existing sockets **A** and **B** is disconnected. A new cable is taken from socket **A** to join three new sockets (**C**, **D** and **E**) installed in the base units. These will supply power to the appliances. New cable must be clipped every 600mm behind the units and chased into the wall where it is above base unit level.

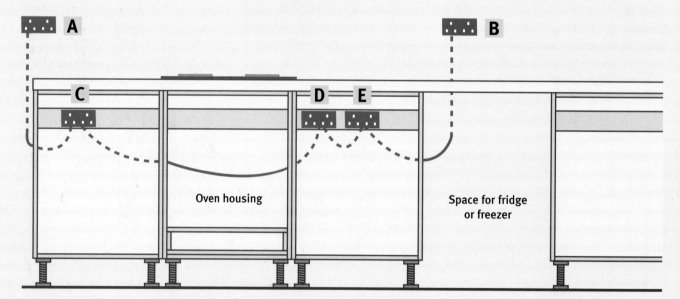

Oven housing

Space for fridge or freezer

Rules for Cookers and Hobs

✔ The electric ignition for a gas cooker or hob must be protected by a 3amp (maximum) cartridge fuse.

✔ A single electric oven rated at 3kW should be connected to the ring main and protected by a 13amp cartridge fuse. It must not be powered from a dedicated 'cooker' circuit unless the fuse at the consumer unit is reduced to 15amp (or 16amp MCB).

✔ Electric ovens rated above 3kW, such as double ovens and some freestanding cookers, should be connected to the cooker supply. They must have an accessible control switch (double pole 45amp, BS3676 or BS4177) fitted within 2 metres and at the consumer unit there must be a fuse rated at 30amp (32amp MCB).

✔ An all-electric hob should be connected to the cooker supply and the same conditions apply as for ovens.

✔ It is permissible to connect an oven over 3kW as well as an all-electric hob to the same cooker supply providing they are both in the same room and the combined rating does not exceed 17.6kW (but only 13.8kW if the control switch incorporates a socket outlet). A control switch must be fitted within 2 metres of each appliance.

✔ If the cooker control switch incorporates a socket outlet it must be protected by an RCD (residual current device) no greater than 30amp.

do it INSTALL AN INTEGRATED SINGLE OVEN

The easiest of all appliances to install is the single oven. The oven is housed in a standard 600mm base unit with a platform fitted on top of two supports. In order to assist ventilation do not fit the back panel when the unit is assembled. A panel matching the cabinet doors should be provided to blank off the cavity below the oven. If this is fitted using spring clips it can be removed to provide access to the space behind.

1 Slide the oven onto the platform **A**. Fix with screws through the sides into the cabinet gables. The screw holes are hidden when the drop-down door is closed **B**. A three-pin plug with a 13amp fuse should be fitted to the cable and plugged into a socket in an adjoining cabinet **C**.

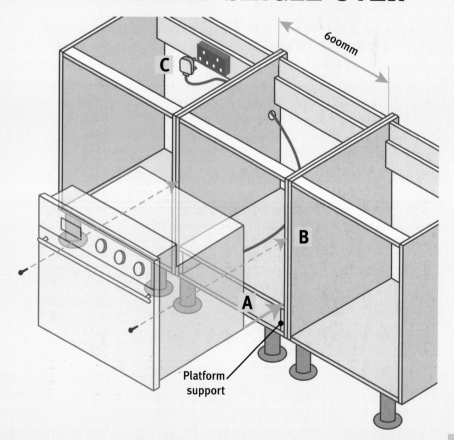

Platform support

Case Study 1: The Finished First-time Buyers' Kitchen

The layout of the finished kitchen is spread along a single wall. To make the most of the small space, the design features space-saving ideas such as integrated appliances and extractor fan, and a draining board that can also be used as a work surface. There is plenty of storage; the shelves either side of the wall cabinets balance the design and make a display space for cookery books and so on.

The dark wood of the worktop, plinth and floor contrast with the white of the units and walls, creating a wraparound effect. Reclaimed materials – such as the Belfast sink and school lab worktop – set off the modern, stainless steel appliances, handles and tap; a good way of combining old and new. The overall effect is fresh, modern and entirely individual.

(Above) The kitchen is now built on a single wall to free up space on the other side. Having appliances integrated where possible ensures the design does not look cluttered.

(Opposite) The dark iroko worktop offsets the bright white of the walls, units and Belfast sink, creating a sleek finish.

Glossary

Butt joint
Used in carpentry; a simple joint where the ends of two parts are simply butted up together with no interlocking parts.

Cam
A metal fitting for assembling carcass panels. Used with metal dowel pins to create a strong, hidden fixing.

Circuit protective conductors (CPC)
The earth core of a cable used to connect exposed conductive parts to the main earthing terminal.

Compression joint
A plumbing joint where a nut forces a gland into close contact with a pipe to form a watertight connection.

Conduit
Plastic or metal protective sheathing for electric cables, usually buried in walls under plaster.

Consumer unit
A box placed after the electricity meter and containing fuses or breakers which split up the supply into separate feeds to supply all the electrical circuits in the house. Modern consumer units must contain miniature circuit breakers (MCBs) and a residual current device (RCD).

Cornice
A length of moulded projecting trim fitted around the top of wall units and tall cabinets.

Coupling
Used in plumbing, this is a straight fitting for connecting plastic or copper pipes in line.

Datum line
A horizontal line used as the basis for setting out other measurements.

Decor panel
Used to cover exposed carcass gables and matched to the door and drawer fronts.

Dry-lining
Plasterboard attached to a wall with plaster dabs.

Elbow
A plumbing connection used to change the direction of a pipe – usually 45° or 90°.

End support panel (ESP)
Used to take the weight of the worktop, such as either side of an appliance, when there is no base unit in place.

First fix
The early stages of plumbing or electrical jobs, such as preparing the route for pipes or wires.

Flux
A substance applied to copper pipe when making a soldered joint. It allows the solder to adhere to the pipe under high temperature when using a blowtorch.

Foam gasket
A foam rubber gasket is used to create a watertight seal between a sink and a worktop.

Fused connection unit (FCU)
An electrical accessory incorporating a cartridge fuse and sometimes a switch. Used to connect appliances directly into a ring main instead of using a fused plug and socket.

Gable
The side panel of a carcass.

Gate valve
A shut-off valve used on low-pressure water pipes such as the outlet pipes from a water tank.

Isolating valve
A plumbing fitting used to stop the flow of water to a section of pipe or an appliance.

Junction box
A box used to enclose a joint in electrical cables.

Miniature circuit breaker (MCB)
A safety trip switch designed to break the circuit in the event of an electrical fault. MCBs are the replacement of fuses in modern consumer units.

Olive
A copper or brass ring used to create a watertight seal in a compression joint. It is squashed around the pipe permanently for a secure fit.

Part P

Part P of the Building Regulations relates to electrical safety. Since it came into effect on 1st Janury 2005, only very limited work can be carried out by non-certified people without notification to the local Building Control authority.

Pattress

A surface-mounted electrical box to which either a switchplate or plug sockets are fitted. The terminating wires are safely contained within the box.

Pelmet

Fitted to the bottom of wall units, usually used to hide under-cabinet lighting.

Plinth

A detachable board fitted between the bottom of a base unit and the floor. It is sometimes referred to as a kick board.

Plumb

Perfectly vertical or true; this can be ascertained by using a spirit level or a plumb-bob.

Push-fit

A plumbing fitting designed to create a watertight joint simply by inserting a pipe.

Radial circuit

A 'straight line' circuit that finishes at the last outlet. The cable does not have to return to the consumer unit.

Residual current device (RSD)

An electromechanical safety switch that will turn off the supply if it detects an imbalance in current. Any socket likely to be used to supply portable equipment outdoors should be protected by an RCD.

Ring main

A type of electric circuit where a cable is looped from a fuse or MCB in the consumer unit to a series of plug sockets and FCUs and returned to the same fuse or MCB.

Rising main

The pipe that conveys fresh water from the incoming supply to the storage tank in the loft.

Silicone sealant

A sealing compound that cures without hardening to create a water-repellent joint. Often applied between worktops and the wall and also around sinks.

Soil stack pipe (SSP)

100mm diameter pipe used to carry bathroom effluent to the foul drain.

Solvent-weld

A liquid substance used to make a watertight seal in a plastic waste pipe joint.

Spur

A branch of wiring to serve a new socket that can be taken from a socket or a junction box wired into the ring main.

Standpipe

A vertical waste pipe fitted with a U-trap used to insert the flexible waste hose from a washing machine or a dishwasher.

Stopcock

A shut-off valve used on high-pressure water pipes such as an incoming water supply.

Stud wall

An internal dividing wall made from a timber frame covered in plasterboard.

Tambour unit

A display unit with a pull-down door, often used to keep kettles and toasters tucked out of sight.

Tee

A straight tee piece connects pipes at 90º and can be used to divide or combine the flow of water.

Trap

A U-bend shape waste fitting that prevents back flow of odours by trapping water in the bend which acts as a liquid barrier.

Trunking

Plastic (or metal) sheathing with a removable lid section for housing electrical cables.

Work triangle

The shape made by connecting the three major work areas of a kitchen: the sink, the cooking area and the refrigerator. More trips are made within this triangle than to any other parts of the kitchen.

Suppliers

APPLIANCES

Comet
www.comet.co.uk
www.clearance-comet.co.uk

Currys
www.currys.com

Trade Appliances
www.trade-appliances.co.uk

Tradingpost
www.tradingpost-appliances.co.uk

ARCHITECTURAL SALVAGE & RECLAMATION

Ebay
www.ebay.co.uk

Friday Ad
www.friday-ad.co.uk

Retrouvius
www.retrouvius.com
020 8960 6060

Salvo
www.salvo.co.uk

GENERAL TOOLS & MATERIALS

B&Q
www.diy.com

Screwfix
www.screwfix.com

Wickes
www.wickes.co.uk

KITCHENS

Bulthaup
www.bulthaup.co.uk

Habitat
www.habitat.net/uk

Ikea
www.ikea.co.uk

Kitchen Clinic
www.kitchenclinic.com

Magnet
www.magnet.co.uk

MFI
www.mfi.co.uk
0870 607 5054

Poggenpohl
www.poggenpohl.de

PWS
www.pws.co.uk

PAINT

Farrow and Ball
www.farrow-ball.co.uk

Little Greene Paint Company
www.thelittlegreene.com

PLUMBING SUPPLIES

John Guest Speedfit Ltd
www.speedfit.co.uk
01895 449233

TOOL HIRE

Brandon Tool Hire
www.brandontoolhire.co.uk
0870 514 3391

HSS Hire
www.hss.com
08457 282828

Speedy Hire
www.speedyhire.co.uk
0845 6015129

WORKTOPS

Corian
www.corian.com

Acknowledgements

Dennis Dixon and GMC Publications Ltd would like to thank the following for their help in compiling this book:

I offer my grateful appreciation to all those who have made this book possible. In particular, my wife, Rita, for her tolerance and understanding during long periods left on her own. To Spencer of SJ Pearcey Kitchens who was the catalyst for this journey and has supported me throughout. To brothers Paul and Mark Ibbot of Penthouse Interiors, as well as Andrew Breese, their apprentice, for their forbearance whilst I shadowed them with my camera. To John Catley of Graniti e Marmi for his advice on granite worktops. To Mr and Mrs P H Irons for endless cups of tea whilst I photographed the installation of their new kitchen. To Lisa, Rachel and Dan for allowing me to use their kitchens as case studies.

Ikea
www.ikea.com

John Guest Ltd
www.speedfit.co.uk

PWS Distributors Ltd
www.pws.co.uk

Editorial Assistance
Gill Parris, Dominique Page

Illustration
Gilda Pacitti

Photography
All photography by Anthony Bailey/GMC Publications, and Dennis Dixon, except for the following:

IKEA®
Front and back covers; pages 1 (tl); 9 (m); 10; 11(t); 13(t); 20; 26(r); 33(bl); 40(bl); 42;

PWS Distributors Ltd.
Cover spine; pages 2; 5; 8; 9 (l,r); 11(b); 12; 24; 25; 26(l); 27(r); 29; 30; 31; 33(tl, tr, br); 34; 35; 36; 37; 38; 39; 40(tr); 41; 43; 44; 45; 54; 68; 91; 104; 108; 114(l); 126; 131; 134; 136; 140(b); 141(t); 144

t=top, m=middle, b=bottom, l=left, r=right

Index

To request a full catalogue of GMC titles, please contact:

GMC Publications,
Castle Place,
166 High Street,
Lewes,
East Sussex,
BN7 1XU,
United Kingdom

Tel: 01273 488005
Fax: 01273 402866

www.thegmcgroup.com